EAT.
COOK.
L.A.

EAT.
COOK.
L.A.

NOTES AND RECIPES FROM THE CITY OF ANGELS

ALEKSANDRA CRAPANZANO

Photographs by **RAY KACHATORIAN**

TEN SPEED PRESS
California | New York

TABLE OF CONTENTS

INTRODUCTION

Los Angeles has been the stuff of parody for as long as it's been the stuff of legend. Such is the fate of a city of angels with perfect weather built around the serious business of make-believe.

As a native New Yorker, I'm guilty of no small share of verbal jousting on the subject. The rivalry between New York and Los Angeles has always been fierce and uninhibited, if perhaps less downright nasty than that between San Francisco and L.A. Historically, the battle has manifested itself in many areas of the culture—fashion, manners, beauty, storytelling—save for one. When it came to its food and restaurants, Los Angeles was simply never considered in the same league as the major culinary outposts of the Northeast, let alone in its own state of California. Alice Waters, Thomas Keller, Napa, and Sonoma were synonymous with great food and wine to the north, while Mexican food, with its spice, heat, ceviche and cocktails, ruled to the south. In L.A., however, until quite recently, the well-heeled tended to go to restaurants, not so much to eat as to see and be seen, to flaunt, strut, and make deals. This was not the restaurant as destination but the restaurant as just another stage set, in a city full of stage sets.

Unless, that is, you drove out beyond the studios to the outskirts of the city and ate the incredible food being cooked in the vast, vibrant world of the immigrants, in the taquerias and Korean barbecue joints and fried-chicken shacks and dumpling houses there. Food that, for the most part, the majority of Angelenos living in the more central parts of the city didn't even know existed. But that's another story, and not the one I'm writing.

I first started going out to Los Angeles regularly after graduate school, armed with an expensive and useless MFA in film directing and a spec script that found the attention of a powerful Hollywood agent. Said agent signed me, then wined and dined me expensively on steak, steamed spinach, and martinis for dinner and chopped salads for lunch. I quickly learned that in Tinseltown, carbs were for losers and butter was a crime. Which was okay for a little while, because the people-watching was fabulous and highly distracting. It was also, I came to understand, not a sport for the meek. So thank God for that steak, though, on second thought, hold the béarnaise.

And then my son Garrick was born, and I found I had a powerful urge to nest (which, though it rhymes with *rest*, turned out to be rather the opposite sort of verb). As if on cue, the Writers Guild went on strike, and Hollywood all but shut down for several months. It was during this time that I did something I'd always dreamed of doing—I wrote my first article, and it was, to no one's surprise who knew me, about food. Amanda Hesser, the food editor at the *New York Times Magazine* at the time, published it and asked me to write more. Food, food writing, cooking, and cookbooks—these had always been great loves of mine, and what began as a lark quickly blossomed into a side career. For a few years, my trips west became sporadic, but this only made what time I did spend in L.A. all the more vivid. With each new trip, the city's changes revealed themselves to me in the stark relief that is only apparent to visitors. And what I saw was thrilling: The city's culinary landscape was all but exploding with energy and vitality. Good restaurants, really good restaurants, seemed literally to pop up across L.A. as if armies of underground chefs were tunneling under the canyons and tar pits, the freeways and valleys.

For a writer, it was impossible not to take note—and notes. I started jotting down restaurant names, tracking chefs, exploring new neighborhoods—Los Feliz, Silver Lake, Highland Park, Boyle Heights, Atwater Village. I started writing articles about dishes I'd eaten in Los Angeles and keeping a journal of dishes I wanted to re-create at home. Moreover, all over La-La Land, I began to hear the rising crescendo of chatter in restaurants, on lines for (impeccably house-roasted) coffee, in bookstores and movie theaters. Food chatter, I mean, with its fan's loquacious urgency, punctuated by moments of silent, sensual memory.

This kind of chatter finds its origin in hungry circles. And by hungry, I don't mean literally hungry, but rather foodie hungry, the kind of appetite for culinary pleasure and satisfaction that for each of us begins with some gateway event, a single taste or meal that triggers desire, longing, and a determination to re-create the contours of such inexpressible joy. This could happen to you in kindergarten or at forty. But once you've had food that hits your pleasure point, you will forever return to its memory. Like Proust's madeleine, it will be a sweet haunting.

This kind of hungry grows. A great meal, then another, and another, and soon the idea of eating anything less than great food starts to make you feel a little bit sad. The good news is that the great food has probably spawned more great food. And just as your palate is singing, so too are the chefs making that great food. And other chefs are catching on. And so is the press. And so are investors. And a cycle is born. And a neighborhood is changed. And then another. And soon an entire city has undergone a culinary revolution.

This is what has happened in Los Angeles. The City of Angels is now sparkling with culinary stardust. It has, in a remarkably short time, transformed itself into the most exciting food city in the United States.

Los Angeles was not the first city I have watched go through such a transformation. In my last book, *The London Cookbook*, I looked at a grand city that had been known for the better part of two thousand years as having the worst food in Western Europe, become, in the short span of two decades, the restaurant capital of Europe. The change was thrilling to witness, delicious to research, and fascinating to investigate.

Los Angeles has a different story. It was a city that had long been almost suspicious of food. It also had a bad case of culinary insecurity. And so, before cooking could become a source of civic excitement and pride, food itself needed to be lifted out of enemy territory. It needed to be looked upon as friend, not foe. Two connected trends led the change brigade: farmers' markets and juicing.

Around 2010, it became terribly chic to roam the Santa Monica and Hollywood farmers' markets with a Provençal basket accessorized, of course, with a bouquet of flowers and a fresh baguette. And, truly, why not? The markets in Los Angeles are glorious. The produce is sun-drenched, richly hued, fragrant, and bountiful. And the season is never-ending. Heirloom tomatoes give way to Meyer lemons, bergamots, and pomelos and, before you know it, the strawberries from Harry's have arrived, and they are indeed exquisite, juicy, and plump. And unlike so much produce in our land of supermarkets, their flavor has depth, making you close your eyes and pay attention. Of course, fresh fruit and vegetables are also good for you. Friend, not foe, as it were. And so, the city began happily nibbling away at its antioxidant-rich purple carrots.

Beauty may not be the only currency in Hollywood, but it is a dominant one. This is no secret to studio executives and no secret to feminists. But it is infinitely more palatable to think of beauty as holistic, rather than as a pat of concealer and brush of blush. How enticing then to learn that nurturing the body with superfoods improves skin tone while also reducing inflammation and fighting cancer. Juicing followed farmers' markets as a trend that promised health, longevity, a cleansed body and soul, and that ever-elusive glow. It tasted good, it felt good; it was good for you and good for the planet. It was not a beverage, it was a way of life that included Pilates and yoga and Headspace. (Full disclosure: I juice. And, yes, "juice" is now a verb.) I still remember the first time, now almost a decade ago, that I wandered into Moon Juice in Venice Beach and tried a spiced sweet potato concoction. It was so beautifully nuanced, so expertly spiced, so elegant. I knew that if I heated it to a simmer, I would have a velvety velouté to serve at dinner. Amanda Chantal Bacon, the

owner of Moon Juice had, in fact, been a classically trained chef before health issues forced her to take a sideways, and highly lucrative, step away from butter and cream. But anyone can juice. If you blend complementary fruits at the peak of their season, you will, more times than not, produce something delicious. The juicing craze hit hard and fast and hasn't dissipated. It has simply evolved into tonics, elixirs, and concentrated immunity shots. But, more importantly, juicing got people hungry. Hungry in that foodie way. It fired up long dormant or virginal taste buds with hits of fiery ginger, floral turmeric root, red hot cayenne pepper, energizing green jalapeño, stimulating cardamom, woody nutmeg, and flirtatious pink peppercorns.

Awake to spices and hungry for more, chefs in Los Angeles started looking to the Middle East for inspiration, and it was not long before virtually every lunch spot was serving hummus and couscous. Homemade harissa made its official debut as a condiment as essential as ketchup and hot sauce. Simultaneously, an awareness of wheat allergies opened up a secret world of grains, which, in turn, led to the now ubiquitous quinoa bowls. And there was little that escaped fermentation, all in the name of happy flora. Meat was no longer guaranteed top billing and even fish was taking a secondary role. Greens, roots, chile peppers, spices, herbs—these were the stars. They might tease with a pretty garland of micro-cilantro flowers or they might taunt with the fiery heat of Thai bird chiles. Either way, they were bound to be bountiful, and they would no doubt surprise with hints of ever more exotic aromas. Because when you remove that centerpiece of meat, you must find other ways to impress and satisfy. You must let your imagination run wild and layer flavors, textures, and colors. You must nourish generously and creatively. This mandate shot a jolt of excitement through the food world. It galvanized a generation of young chefs and sparked a vibrant new cuisine.

Humor me and compare a restaurant dish from L.A. circa 2009— let's go back to that grilled rib eye with steamed spinach—with a dish from 2019, with seared slices of kabocha, smoked paprika labneh, flash-fried shishito peppers, toasted freekeh with preserved lemon zest. It's a remarkable evolution that in a few short years also flipped the restaurant supply chain. The demand was now for fresh, local, seasonal, sustainable, organic, with a premium on esoteric, specialty produce. This shift in appetite transformed surrounding farms—changed what the farmers grew and how they grew it and, in so doing, changed the very soil of Southern California, proving once again that supply and demand at a local level can have a tremendous impact.

While chefs were tending herb gardens and traveling a virtual spice road, the film studios were going through a crisis. The golden age of studios was long over by 2008, but the economic depression irreparably hurt the independent film world, and the subsequent shift to streaming drove a stake through a stunned and unprepared industry. People no longer had much of a reason to spend fifty dollars on movie tickets, popcorn, and overly sweetened soda with too much crushed ice. They could stay in the comfort of their home and watch nearly anything at any time.

What does this have to do with food, you might ask? In a one-industry town, quite a lot. For the better part of the last century, show business had orbited a handful of movie studios, each with its own food ecosystem, replete with a hierarchy of in-house commissaries and nearby restaurants. But as television writing rooms and internet start-ups began populating disparate areas of the city, restaurants soon followed. This new generation of eateries didn't cater to expense accounts and business meetings. You could show up at their doors in flip-flops, laptop in hand, and eat beautiful, healthy food in a casual, sunny space. As the vibe and purpose became more casual, so too did the food. Luxury became ceremonial-grade matcha lattes and wild strawberries with yuzu sugar. It became hand-glazed ceramic bowls and hand-blown water glasses. The luxury was precisely in not putting on that suit, not eating another McCarthy chopped salad at the Polo Lounge surrounded by studio executives and agents.

At the same time, the local art scene was taking off at a furious rate. Los Angeles had always been home to serious collectors, but the relevant galleries had been in New York and New York alone. When the Broad opened its doors in 2015 across the way from MOCA, it cemented downtown's reputation as the arts district. With the Walt Disney Concert Hall, the Microsoft Theater, and the Staples Center in the vicinity, the Arts District started drawing not only locals, but a sophisticated body of tourists and collectors. Art dealers quickly realized that they could open galleries in Los Angeles far more affordably than in New York, while artists began migrating west for larger and more affordable studio space (to say nothing of the weather).

Good food and good art seem to dance in tandem, and it's perhaps no surprise that new restaurants started popping up near the new museums, galleries, and studio spaces. In a parallel migration, chefs from around the country started moving to Los Angeles to open restaurants. Some came with fame and fortune already made; others came to make their mark. All of them came for the sun-ripened fruit, fragrant herbs, and sunny spaces—and for the euphoric sense of possibility. A New York address was suddenly no longer necessary for national or even global recognition. Word of mouth could travel by Instagram, Snapchat, and Twitter faster than the reviews of newspaper critics and the even slower, albeit more in-depth, reporting of magazines.

But the refrain I heard again and again from the many chefs I interviewed for this book was how much they loved the freedom they found in Los Angeles. The American West has always been a land of opportunity, a land of dreams, and most importantly, a land free from the constraints of the Eastern establishment. Nearly every transplanted chef spoke of feeling liberated to experiment with new foods, new flavors, new approaches to everything from a plate of spaghetti to a graffiti-painted wall. The unspoken rules of success in New York, Boston, Washington D.C., and Chicago simply didn't apply. And this burst of creative freedom is evident everywhere in the inspired, vivid, bold new food of the City of Angels.

I wanted to write this book for so many reasons. I wanted to celebrate this sprawling, sunbaked city that I have come to love. I wanted to pay homage to the extraordinary chefs who've turned it into a restaurant mecca. I wanted to witness a city in the throes of culinary love. But the biggest reason of all was to bring you these amazing recipes. So let me tell you what to expect in *EAT. COOK. L.A.*

The food is fresh, prepared simply, presented simply, and tends to feature an abundance of herbs, spice, and color. The pantry is global, but most everything is easily found online, if not in a nearby market. As chefs have leaned into simpler cooking, they've focused more on deepening flavors and adding textures and nuance. This approach easily lends itself to home cooks and requires no special techniques, equipment, or training. The recipes in this book come from chefs, but ironically I've chosen them precisely because they don't feel like chef recipes. I simply love to cook and eat them, and I think you will too.

What this book does not include is threefold. I've avoided fancy fare requiring a restaurant staff. There are so many extraordinary restaurants in Los Angeles that serve food that simply can't be re-created at home, and so, with a bit of a heavy heart, I've left out restaurants such as Vespertine, Providence, Spring, and Trois Mec. It's also my firm belief that homemade bread, ramen, pizza dough, sushi, tortillas, ravioli, and charcuterie deserve their own cookbooks written by their own masters. And so you will see an absence in these pages of these delicacies, however quotidian they may be to Angelenos. Los Angeles has the highest concentration of immigrant cuisine in the U.S., very well worth its own series of books, television shows, and repeated visits. Korean, Mexican, Chinese, Filipino, Guatemalan, Iranian—these cuisines are thriving. To do them justice would

require an expertise I don't profess to have as well as long lists of ingredients that many of us can't easily find. If you're in Los Angeles, I urge you to seek out the best of these authentic restaurants, cafes, shops, and food trucks. You will be amazed.

With *EAT. COOK. L.A.,* I've taken a cue from the way the city eats and organized it accordingly. Angelenos, I discovered, like breakfast. They like to graze. They like ice cream—a lot. They make awesome cocktails. Sitting down to a three-course meal tends to happen at night, in winter. Most meals are casual and unstructured, and much of the food can be eaten at any time of day. Organizing this cookbook traditionally, beginning with appetizers and including sequential chapters on fish, foul, meat, and so on didn't, I quickly realized, fit the pulse of the city. A breakfast bowl at teatime makes sense if you want it then, and a plate of crudo at midnight sounds like just the thing. Why not spike a latte at brunch and carry banh mi sandwiches to the beach at sunset? Or have a protein-packed bowl of lentils and salsa verde in the afternoon when your energy wanes. The correct order of a meal here is however you decide to make it. Stuffy notions of formal dinners are not for the wide-open, light-filled future-present tense of today's Los Angeles. But please do put flowers on your salad, saffron in your lemonade, and once in a while, make sure to eat ice cream for supper.

A FEW NOTES ON INGREDIENTS

I am not a fussy cook, but I do hold myself to these ten commandments, as they often make the difference between good food and great. One of them is homemade stock. Make it in big batches and keep a few containers on hand in the freezer. Another is Parmesan. Buy it in large wedges and grate it, as needed, in a food processor. I use a Microplane grater for zesting citrus as well as for mincing garlic. I use scissors to snip fresh herbs and nearly everything else. If you have ready access to milk and cream that is not ultrapasteurized, do use it. It will be fresher and creamier than those with far-reaching expiration dates.

When baking, I fluff up the flour a bit before measuring it in metal measuring cups and leveling the top off with the back of a knife.

When precision is called for, I've added weights. But, for the most part, these recipes are forgiving and meant to be cooked with ease, confidence, and pleasure.

Unless otherwise noted, assume the following ten commandments hold sway:

1. Salt is either Maldon, Himalayan, fleur de sel, or sel gris, unless salting water or otherwise specified.

2. Pepper is black pepper, freshly ground.

3. Eggs are large and organic.

4. Butter is unsalted.

5. Stock is homemade, when possible.

6. Parmesan is freshly grated.

7. Olive oil is extra-virgin.

8. Sherry and balsamic vinegars are aged and unadulterated.

9. Citrus is organic whenever zested.

10. Cooking wine is good enough to drink.

On Salt

Keep a jar of fleur de sel, a box of Maldon sea salt flakes, and a grinder of pink Himalayan salt on hand. Use what and how much feels right to you. A basic sea salt is fine for salting water and stock, but that last pinch or grinding of a good finishing salt matters. So, too, does the size. Maldon sea salt flakes tease the palate with a light, dissolving texture. Fleur de sel refines, as it seasons with discreet persuasion.

Note: If you are pregnant or have a compromised immune system, avoid all raw or undercooked eggs. And, apologies, but crudo and all raw fish and meat is off the table too.

BREAKFAST
ANYTIME OF DAY

CORNMEAL PANCAKES WITH TURMERIC YUZU BUTTER

These pancakes can swing sweet, topped with maple syrup, or savory, as Centeno serves them at P.Y.T., with a vibrant turmeric yuzu butter. Or try them topped with date butter, which is as simple as combining one cup of softened butter with a quarter cup of pitted dates in a food processor and blending until well combined.

1 cup coarse-ground polenta (preferably from Anson Mills)

½ cup all-purpose flour

½ cup pastry flour

1 teaspoon salt

½ teaspoon baking soda

¼ teaspoon baking powder

1 cup buttermilk

½ cup butter, melted

¼ cup sugar

¼ cup honey

1 egg

additional butter for cooking

turmeric yuzu butter, for serving (see recipe)

Serves 4

In a large bowl, mix the polenta, all-purpose flour, pastry flour, salt, baking soda, baking powder, buttermilk, melted butter, sugar, honey, and egg until blended. Set aside in the refrigerator to rest for half an hour.

Heat a pat of butter over medium-high heat in a large nonstick pan until sizzling. Drop spoonfuls of batter into the pan and cook the pancakes until they start to brown at the edges and bubbles start to form on their surface, 2 to 3 minutes. Flip and cook the other side until golden, another 2 to 3 minutes. Serve with turmeric yuzu butter.

Turmeric Yuzu Butter Makes a little more than 1 cup

1 cup butter, at room temperature

2½ teaspoons grated fresh turmeric root

1 teaspoon yuzu juice or 1 tablespoon freshly squeezed Meyer lemon juice

pinch of salt

pinch of sugar

Blend all of the ingredients in a food processor until fully integrated. The butter may be stored in the refrigerator for up to 3 days.

WHAT YOU NEED TO KNOW

Fresh turmeric root has floral and citrus notes, and it is packed with anti-inflammatories. When handling it, use gloves or it will stain your fingers yellow. The turmeric yuzu butter is also delicious on fish and couscous.

RICOTTA AND CHÈVRE FRITTERS WITH SAFFRON HONEY

These are ridiculously easy to consume with abandon. Comforting in the morning, they also deserve a second sighting at cocktail hour with a glass or two of Prosecco or Cava.

HONEY SAUCE

1 tablespoon hot water

6 strands saffron

¼ cup honey

pinch of salt

RICOTTA FRITTERS

1½ cups fresh ricotta

½ cup fresh goat cheese

¼ cup grated Pecorino Romano

2 tablespoons minced fresh chives

1 egg

¼ cup panko

vegetable oil, for frying

maldon sea salt

Serves 4

To make the honey sauce, gently mix the hot water with the saffron in a small bowl and let sit 5 to 10 seconds. Put the honey, salt, and water with saffron in a small saucepan and warm over medium heat; stir to combine. When the honey is warm, remove from the heat and set aside.

To make the ricotta fritters, in a large bowl, mix together the ricotta, goat cheese, Pecorino Romano, 1 tablespoon of the chives, and the egg until combined and let rest for 10 minutes in the fridge.

Put the panko in a shallow bowl. Using a small ice cream scoop, shape the ricotta mixture into spheres and put them on a baking sheet lined with parchment paper. One by one, roll each of the spheres in the panko to coat completely and return to the sheet.

Pour enough oil into a large heavy pot so that it comes up the sides at least an inch. Heat over medium-high heat until the oil reaches 350°F on a deep-fry thermometer. Alternatively, insert the handle of a wooden spoon into the oil so that it touches the bottom of the pan. If small bubbles come up the sides of the spoon, the oil is hot enough.

Working in batches, using a large metal spoon, carefully place the ricotta fritters in the hot oil. Fry until golden on the bottom and, using two spoons, flip the fritters over. Cook until golden brown. This entire process should take 3 to 5 minutes. Transfer to a plate lined with paper towels to drain the oil.

Drizzle with the honey sauce and sprinkle with Maldon sea salt and the remaining 1 tablespoon of chives. Serve immediately.

WHAT YOU NEED TO KNOW

I am a coward when it comes to frying foods. Oil that hot makes me beat a hasty retreat. My solution is to use a Le Creuset or Staub Dutch oven. The high sides work like an impenetrable fortress and, in this case, I like to be on the outside. That, mitts, and a long-handled spoon. When I don't have saffron on hand, I like serving these with a drizzle of hot chile-infused honey, available in gourmet markets and online. About ricotta: This recipe begs for a relatively thick ricotta, preferably artisanal or homemade. If you use the supermarket variety in a tub, drain it over a cheesecloth or muslin-lined sieve overnight and discard the excess liquid. Too wet a ricotta will make your fritters soggy. But a good, rich ricotta will lead to a thing of bliss.

EGG SLUT

This little coddled egg is the stuff of cravings, which may explain the hour-long wait to order one come Sunday mornings. The Slut, as it is called, with a sardonic nod to political correctness, is simply a cage-free coddled egg placed on top of a smooth potato puree, poached in a glass jar, topped with a shower of really good gray sea salt and snipped fresh chives, and served with a length of toasted baguette. It is the taste of luxury. The taste of luxury begets a hunger for more luxury, and so it is perhaps no wonder that I took this over the top one day and made my own version: the Caviar Slut. Prepare as described below, then dollop with a spoonful of caviar just before serving. It doesn't need to be an extravagant caviar—just a teaspoon of salmon roe is enough to give this a salty sea breeze.

3 tablespoons sea salt

1 pound russet potatoes, peeled and cut into 1-inch cubes

10 tablespoons butter, cut into pieces

1 baguette

4 eggs

2 tablespoons thinly sliced chives

gray sea salt

Serves 4

Fill a pot with water and the sea salt and bring to a boil over high heat. Add the potatoes and cook at a lively simmer until they are fork-tender, 15 to 20 minutes. Drain and press through a food mill or potato ricer. Stir in the butter and season with salt to taste. Fill four heatproof jars with the potato puree.

Meanwhile, bring a kettle of water to a boil. Cut the baguette into fourths. Then halve each fourth and set aside to toast at the last minute.

Place a saucepan on the stove. Set the jars of puree in the saucepan and crack an egg into each one. Cover with the lids. Pour the boiling water into the saucepan to create a bain-marie. The water should come about three-quarters of the way up the jars. Set over a medium-low heat to return the water to a simmer and keep it simmering until the egg whites are set and the yolks are almost set, but still slightly runny, about 15 minutes. Remove from the heat.

Serve immediately, with a shower of chives and gray sea salt. The toasted baguette makes an edible spoon, but you'll want a little spoon as well for the hard-to-reach spots.

WHAT YOU NEED TO KNOW

You will want to use lidded ½-pint mason jars to make a slut. Weck makes a good one, easily purchased online. But any heatproof lidded jar that holds between 5 and 8 ounces will work. If you are pressed for time, you may repurpose the potato-cooking water as a bain-marie. A little starch from the potatoes may get on the outside of the jar, which is easily wiped off. For a more pristine appearance, use fresh water to make the bain-marie.

Emily Fiffer and Heather Sperling of Botanica, Silver Lake

MARKET FRUIT AND GRAIN BREAKFAST BOWL

Grain bowl recipes abound, but this one deserves special attention. By adding a few extra steps, Fiffer and Sperling have hit on what I consider to be the ideal recipe. They cook three different grains separately, then simmer them together in aromatic-infused coconut milk. Anise, vanilla, and cinnamon tease the palate awake; coconut milk offers the gentle comfort one seeks in the morning; and a jammy compote offers a burst of color and a hit of sweet fruit.

GRAIN BASE

1 cup black rice, soaked overnight and then cooked

1 cup wheatberries, soaked overnight and then cooked

1 cup cooked quinoa

1 cup water

4 cups full-fat coconut milk

2 star anise pods, whizzed to a powder in a spice grinder

2 vanilla beans, split lengthwise, scraped, beans and pods reserved

1 teaspoon ground cinnamon

zest and juice of 2 oranges (preferably Cara Cara)

2 teaspoons Maldon sea salt

TO SERVE

strawberry compote (see recipe)

fresh berries

full-fat coconut milk

zest from about 2 large oranges

Serves 6

To make the grain base, combine all of the ingredients in a saucepan and bring to a simmer over low heat. Cook, stirring frequently, until the mixture softens and thickens, about 20 minutes. The wheatberries should still have some chew to them, but not offer an unpleasant resistance. Remove the vanilla beans.

Divide the mixture among individual bowls and serve with a large dollop of compote, a handful of fresh berries, a drizzle of coconut milk, and a faint shower of orange zest.

WHAT YOU NEED TO KNOW

Cook the grains according to the instructions on their package. You may substitute alternate grains, such as farro, freekeh, barley, or use whole oats. If time is short, simply use one grain. Mornings are for bending the rules. But it's also possible to make the grains a day in advance and reheat them in a double boiler or microwave. Leftover compote is terrific on yogurt.

Strawberry Compote

2 overflowing pints fresh strawberries, hulled and halved

2 star anise pods

2 vanilla beans, split lengthwise, scraped, beans and pods reserved

zest and juice of 2 oranges (preferably Cara Cara)

zest and juice of 2 lemons (preferably Meyer)

½ cup white wine

1 to 2 tablespoons maple syrup, to taste

pinch of salt

Preheat the oven to 350°F.

Toss all of the ingredients into a baking dish and stir well. Bake for 40 minutes, checking every 15 minutes to stir. Add a splash of water if the mixture appears dry. The texture should be that of a loose jam.

Remove the vanilla bean and star anise pods. The compote may be served warm or at room temperature. It's even good chilled. Store in a glass jar in the refrigerator for up to 3 days.

HONEY RAISIN OATCAKES

Based on Scottish oatcakes, these superhealthy fiber, flaxseed, oat, and carrot-packed beauties make a healthy breakfast for the champion on the go.

2 tablespoons butter, at room temperature, plus 10 tablespoons butter, cut into ¼-inch dice and chilled

1¾ cups old-fashioned rolled oats

1 medium carrot, peeled and shredded

1 cup plus 2 tablespoons all-purpose flour

6 tablespoons semolina flour

3 tablespoons light brown sugar

1⅛ teaspoons baking soda

1½ teaspoons salt

6 tablespoons buttermilk

6 tablespoons honey

6 tablespoons golden raisins

3 tablespoons whole flaxseeds

1 egg, for wash

_____

Serves 6

WHAT YOU NEED TO KNOW

These are not cakes as we know them in the U.S., but rather a cross between a cookie and a scone, meant, originally, to be stored in a lunch tin while you roamed the Scottish moors. All to say, don't serve them for dessert. They don't need spice, but if you make them repeatedly and want a variation, try adding half a teaspoon of cinnamon or swapping the raisins for minced candied ginger or chopped dried apricots. They may also be taken savory and served with butter and Cheddar, for example. Don't worry that the recipe doesn't call for eggs. Butter and buttermilk bind the pastry. Store the oatcakes in a tin, not a plastic bag, or they will lose their crisp exterior. They are best served warm, within a day.

Preheat the oven to 375°F. Butter a 6-cup muffin pan with the 2 tablespoons room-temperature butter.

Place 1½ cups of the oats and all of the shredded carrot into a food processor and process into a coarse meal. If you have a large food processor, continue to use it. Otherwise transfer the ingredients to a large mixing bowl and use a handheld electric mixer or a stand mixer fitted with the paddle attachment. Add the all-purpose flour, semolina flour, brown sugar, baking soda, and salt and mix on low speed just to combine.

Add the chilled butter and continue to mix on low speed until pea-size lumps form, about 1 minute. Add the buttermilk and honey and pulse until just incorporated. Do not overmix. Transfer the batter to a large mixing bowl and fold in the raisins and flaxseeds.

Spoon ½ cup of dough into each muffin mold. Do not press down on the dough; leave it craggy. In a small bowl, beat the egg. Brush the top of each muffin lightly with the egg wash and sprinkle with the remaining ¼ cup of oats.

Bake, rotating halfway through, until golden brown, about 30 minutes. Invert the muffin pan on a cooling rack to unmold. Let the oatcakes cool slightly while upside down so that their exteriors will be crunchy. Serve while still warm.

ICED SPIKED LATTE

This is a somewhat healthy, somewhat bacchanal and very delicious way to drink coffee, ideal for a lazy brunch with friends. Fernet-Branca, the bitter herbal liqueur, is said to cure hangovers. Blended with rum, cold brew, dates, coconut milk, and ice, this so-called latte stirs the mind awake with the liqueur's twenty-seven mysterious ingredients, while the rum keeps any urgency in check.

1 ounce spiked cold brew (see recipe)

2 ounces coconut-date milk (see recipe)

2 ice cubes

Serves 1

Spiked Cold Brew Makes 4 cups

6 tablespoons ground espresso

2 cups Fernet-Branca

2 cups rum (preferably Gosling's Black Seal)

Coconut-Date Milk Makes 6 cups

2 cups full-fat coconut milk

2 cups simmering water

6 dates, pitted

2 cups cold water

WHAT YOU NEED TO KNOW

This is a cold drink. Tempting as it might be to try, it doesn't heat well. The cold brew needs twenty-four hours to steep. The quantities of spiked cold brew and coconut-date milk here make enough for about twenty lattes, which should roughly serve a party of ten.

Place the cold brew, coconut-date milk, and ice in a blender and blend until smooth. Or combine the brew and milk and serve on the rocks.

Stir together the espresso grounds, Fernet, and rum in a glass jar and let steep for 24 hours. Strain through a fine-mesh sieve. Refrigerate for up to 3 days, stored in a sealed glass jar.

Combine the coconut milk, simmering water, and dates in a bowl and let sit for approximately 20 minutes. Transfer to a blender. Add the cold water and blend until entirely smooth. Strain through a fine-mesh sieve or chinois. Refrigerate for up to 4 days, stored in a sealed glass jar.

Eamon Kelly of Rose Café, Venice Beach

HIGHLAND ICED COFFEE

Caffeine talks back.

2 ounces cold-brew coffee

1½ ounces reposado tequila (preferably Ocho)

½ ounce chile liqueur (such as Ancho Reyes)

½ ounce simple syrup

3 coffee beans (optional)

Serves 1

In an ice-filled cocktail shaker, combine the coffee, tequila, chile liqueur, and simple syrup and shake for 20 seconds. Strain into a chilled Collins or old-fashioned glass. Top with coffee beans.

BREAKFAST PIZZA

American bacon, eggs, and potatoes wake up in Italy to rosemary, Parmesan, and a drizzle of really good olive oil.

table salt for cooking the potatoes

2 large peeled Yukon gold potatoes

maldon sea salt

freshly cracked pepper

enough pizza dough for two 8- to 10-inch pizzas

extra-virgin olive oil, as needed

½ cup thinly sliced red onion

12 very thin slices of bacon

2 tablespoons fresh rosemary leaves, chopped

½ cup grated Parmesan

2 eggs

———

Serves 2

Preheat the oven to 500°F. If using, preheat 2 pizza stones.

Fill a pot with water, add salt, and bring to a boil over high heat. Add the potatoes and boil until easily pierced with a knife, 20 to 30 minutes. Drain the potatoes and set aside to cool to room temperature. Once cool, grate the potatoes using a box grater. Season with salt and pepper.

Divide the pizza dough in half. Stretch each piece of dough into a circle, 8 to 10 inches in diameter. Place the two circles of dough on a baking sheet or pizza peel and brush with olive oil.

Divide the ingredients between the two dough rounds in this order: potatoes, onion, bacon, and rosemary. Sprinkle each pizza with 2 tablespoons of the Parmesan and bake for 5 minutes. (If using a pizza stone, slide the pizzas onto the stone, using the pizza peel.) Remove the pizzas. Crack an egg in the center of each pizza. Return to the oven for another 3 minutes, or until the yolks are set.

Brush the outer edge of the crust with olive oil and drizzle the whole pizzas with a bit more olive oil. Sprinkle with Maldon salt, cracked pepper, and the remaining ¼ cup Parmesan. Serve immediately.

WHAT YOU NEED TO KNOW

Most grocery stores sell frozen or refrigerated pizza dough, so no worries if you don't have the time to make your own. This recipe is flexible, but assume you want to end up with two 8- to 10-inch pizzas and buy or make dough accordingly. The potatoes may be cooked ahead of time and kept refrigerated.

BREAKFAST BURRITO WITH HOMEMADE CHORIZO

Already a legend, these burritos are for those mornings when you crave heat, meat, spice, and sustenance.

6 large russet potatoes, peeled and cut into cubes

4 tablespoons kosher salt

3 guajillo chiles

1 pound leaf lard or pork fat, cut into cubes

1 pound ground pork meat—from the shoulder or leg

8 garlic cloves, minced

3 tablespoons paprika

2 tablespoons crumbled chiles de arbol

2 teaspoons freshly ground black pepper

2 teaspoons dried oregano

2 teaspoons ground cumin

1 teaspoon ground cloves

1 teaspoon ground coriander

½ cup distilled white vinegar

6 burrito-size flour tortillas

6 fried eggs or 12 scrambled eggs (optional)

chives, snipped, for serving

Serves 6

WHAT YOU NEED TO KNOW

The eggs—they're optional, but good. A fried egg gives you that warm, runny thing. Scrambled eggs offset the spice and texture of the homemade chorizo, making the burrito less intense but more nuanced. The chorizo may be made up to two days in advance. When making this for kids, try adding a few spoonfuls of cooked rice, sour cream, or hash browns to temper the chile heat.

Place the potatoes in a large stockpot and add enough cold water to cover. Set the pot over high heat. When the water comes to a simmer, add 2 tablespoons of the salt and cook the potatoes until they are fork-tender, about 15 minutes. Drain and set aside.

To make the chorizo, combine the guajillos with a cup or two of water in a small saucepan over high heat. Cook until the guajillos are soft, about 5 minutes. Remove from the heat and let come to room temperature. When the guajillos are cool enough to handle, drain them and remove and discard their stems and seeds.

In a food processor, pulse the lard a few times. Add the pork bit by bit, while continuing to pulse, until the pork and lard are finely ground and have the texture of pâté, coarse but very spreadable. Add the garlic, paprika, crumbled chiles de arbol, the remaining 2 tablespoons salt, the pepper, oregano, cumin, cloves, coriander, and vinegar and pulse to blend.

You may make the chorizo up to 1 day in advance and store it in the fridge, wrapped tightly in plastic wrap. Bring it to room temperature before proceeding.

In a heavy skillet, cook the chorizo over medium-high heat, breaking it up with the back of a wooden spoon to render the fat. Add the potatoes and let them cook until they start to form a bit of a crust on the bottom, about 6 minutes. Flip and remove from the heat.

In a separate dry skillet, warm the tortillas until hot but not crispy. Assemble the burritos with as much of the chorizo as you like and the eggs, if using. Sprinkle with chives and fold. Serve immediately with lots of napkins!

Jessica Koslow of Sqirl, Silver Lake

BROWN RICE PORRIDGE WITH PISTACHIOS, APRICOT JAM, AND GREEN CARDAMOM

On my last visit to Sqirl, a version of this porridge, topped with hazelnuts and a delicious raspberry cardamom jam, was on the menu. I cannot refuse anything with cardamom. It is a spice that makes me smile, pure and simple. There's even evidence to be found that it is, in fact, a stimulant. It makes sense, then, that I would want to wake up to the smell of this fragrant pod . . . in greater abundance. And so, at home, I started sprinkling this rice porridge with freshly ground green cardamom. Pistachios and apricot jam were my next additions. All to say, use the porridge recipe as a base and then fiddle with it to your heart's content. For my son, Garrick, this means a large dollop of vivid red strawberry jam. For my husband, John, it means the beach plum jam he grew up eating on Nantucket in the summer.

1 cup medium-grain brown rice or white Arborio

4 cups whole milk, plus a little extra to splash on at the end

4 cups water

¼ cup sugar

½ teaspoon fleur de sel

½ teaspoon vanilla extract

⅓ cup chopped pistachios

freshly ground green cardamom, to taste

apricot jam, to taste

Serves 3 or 4

Rinse the rice in a fine-mesh sieve with cold water until it runs clear. Combine the rice, milk, water, sugar, salt, and vanilla in a heavy saucepan. Bring the liquid to a boil over medium-high heat and continue to cook at a lively simmer, stirring occasionally, until the rice is soft, the porridge is thick, and much of the liquid has evaporated. This will take a solid hour.

Serve immediately in wide bowls, topped with the pistachios, cardamom, and a generous dollop of jam. If you'd like, add a splash of milk to loosen the porridge a bit or pass a milk pitcher at the table.

WHAT YOU NEED TO KNOW

This takes an hour to make, and most of us haven't got that kind of time in the chaos of the weekday morning rush. It is, however, easily made in advance and reheated. Use a microwave or a double boiler. Simply add a little extra milk if the porridge has become too thick. And, of course, wait to add the toppings until the last minute.

DAHL, PERSIAN LIME, YOGURT, HONEY
BRAISED GREENS, POACHED EGGS
LONG TOAST   13.

AVOCADO TOAST

JJ'S AVOCADOS, HOT PICKLED
CARROTS, GREEN GARLIC
CRÈME FRAÎCHE, WOOD
SORREL, HOUSE ZA'ATAR (V) 9.50

6.

TOMATO AND CORRIANDER JAM
MELTED BEECHERS CHEDDAR
ARUGULA

THE WOODSTOCK

PULLED CHICKEN, SHREDDED VEG.
SPROUTS, SUNFLOWER TAHINI ON
BUB AND GRANDMA'S COUNTRY   12.

THE FULL MONTE   15.
(ADD AVOCADO)

Margarita and Walter Manzke of République, La Brea

GREEN TEA BASIL SMASH

For hot mornings when the sun is already bright and urging you forth into the day, this iced matcha will tease you awake with flirting notes of basil, pineapple, and lime.

1½ teaspoons matcha powder

1 cup simmering water

3 or 4 fresh basil leaves

¼ cup fresh pineapple chunks

1½ ounces simple syrup

½ ounce freshly squeezed lime juice

2 slices of lime

club soda or sparkling water, for finishing

crystallized ginger, for garnish (optional)

Serves 1

Combine the matcha powder with the simmering water in a bowl and whisk until thoroughly blended. Let cool to room temperature, then refrigerate until cold.

Combine the basil, pineapple, simple syrup, lime juice, chilled matcha, and lime slices in an ice-filled cocktail shaker, muddling them together. Shake for 20 seconds, then strain into an ice-filled Collins glass. Top with club soda. Garnish with crystallized ginger.

WHAT YOU NEED TO KNOW

To make simple syrup, simply bring an equal amount of water and sugar to a boil. Stir to dissolve the sugar. Set aside to cool. Keep refrigerated until ready to use.

RÉPUBLIQUE

République thrums with a contented buzz from morning to night, but my favorite time to be there is early morning. I like to perch on a stool at one of the tables up front, near the tall windows, and bask in the morning sun with a Green Tea Basil Smash (page 45). Built in 1928 for Charlie Chaplin, the building on South La Brea Boulevard went on to have a storied culinary history. Before Walter and Margarita Manzke took over the space in 2013, it had, from 1989 to 2012, been home to Nancy Silverton and Mark Peel's seminal restaurant, Campanile (see page 118). Proof, perhaps, that there's a bit of charm in certain buildings as elusive as the timing of a mime or the palate of a chef.

Jessica Koslow of Sqirl, Silver Lake

TODDY TONIC

This is the way to start a winter's day when the body craves heat in both spice and temperature. At night, spike it with a shot of warmed rum, brandy, or Calvados for a true toddy.

6 whole cloves

2 cups apple juice

½ teaspoon ground ginger

½ teaspoon ground turmeric

½ teaspoon ground cinnamon

¼ teaspoon freshly ground black pepper

1 teaspoon cardamom ghee (see recipe; optional)

Gently heat the cloves in a small pan for for a few minutes to release their essential oils.

Pour the apple juice into a saucepan and warm over medium-high heat. Add the cloves, ginger, turmeric, cinnamon, and pepper to the juice and bring to a boil. Lower the heat to a bare simmer and let the mixture steep for 5 minutes.

Strain and serve hot. If you are using the cardamom ghee, add ½ teaspoon of it to each hot drink. Stir and enjoy.

———

Serves 2

Cardamom Ghee Makes ¼ cup

¼ cup ghee

½ teaspoon ground cardamom

Warm the ghee in a small pot over medium heat. Once it begins to liquefy, add the cardamom. Turn the heat to low and let the mixture steep for 5 minutes. The ghee may be cooled and kept refrigerated in a glass jar for up to a month.

KALE MARY

Mary, on a green kick.

2 ounces blanco tequila (preferably Arette)

2½ ounces green mix (see recipe)

½ ounce freshly squeezed lemon juice

¼ ounce agave syrup

2 asparagus spears, for garnish

1 olive on a toothpick, for garnish

Chill a Collins glass. Combine the tequila, green mix, lemon juice, and agave in a chilled, ice-filled shaker. Roll back and forth a few times; don't shake, as no aeration is needed. Roll the liquid ingredients into the glass, then back into the shaker, and back into the glass. Garnish with the asparagus spears and olive.

Serves 1

Green Mix

6 green tomatoes, such as Green Zebra, cored, halved, and sliced

2 tablespoons olive oil

salt and pepper

1 head celery, chopped

1 bunch kale, stems discarded, leaves chopped

2 teaspoons grated Parmesan

½ jalapeño chile, seeded

Preheat the oven to 375°F.

Lightly toss the tomatoes with the olive oil and season with salt and pepper. Spread them out on a baking sheet and roast for 20 to 25 minutes. Set aside to cool to room temperature.

Combine the celery and kale in a high-speed blender and pulse to break down. Add 4 teaspoons salt, 2 teaspoons pepper, the Parmesan, and jalapeño and blend very well. Add the roasted tomatoes and blend again until perfectly smooth. Refrigerate until ready to use.

David Lentz of the Hungry Cat, Hollywood

THE THIRSTY CAT BLOODY MARY

Bloody Mary recipes are like chocolate chip cookie recipes: you think you don't need another, only to find yourself flirting with a newcomer. Chef Lentz's secret, here, is in roasting half of the tomatoes before juicing them.

2 ounces vodka

½ ounce spice mix (see recipe), or a bit more if you like spice

4 ounces tomato juice (see recipe)

1 lemon wedge

1 lime wedge

fresh horseradish root, for garnish

Serves 1

Pour the vodka, spice mix, and tomato juice into an ice-filled Collins glass and stir. Garnish with the lemon and lime wedges. Using a Microplane, give the drink 5 or 6 gratings of horseradish.

WHAT YOU NEED TO KNOW

The tomatoes need a night of marinating. I like to double the roasted tomatoes and freeze half for another day. They can be frozen for up two months.

Spice Mix

4 ounces olive oil

1½ ounces Worcestershire sauce

1½ ounces freshly squeezed lemon juice

1¾ teaspoons Tabasco

2 ounces freshly grated horseradish root

4 teaspoons freshly ground black pepper

1¾ teaspoons sugar

1¾ teaspoons celery seeds, ground

1¾ teaspoons kosher salt

1 teaspoon garlic powder

Combine all of the ingredients in a bowl and stir well to combine.

Tomato Juice

10 ripe good-quality tomatoes (such as Early Girl)

olive oil, as needed

kosher salt and freshly ground black pepper

Cut the tomatoes in half and core them. Discard the seeds. Toss with the oil and season with salt and pepper. Marinate overnight in a cool spot; do not refrigerate, or the tomatoes will lose their flavor.

The following day, preheat the oven to 425°F. Divide the tomatoes in half. Roast half of the tomatoes until just starting to char, about 15 minutes. Set aside to cool.

Transfer the roasted tomatoes to a blender. Using a slotted spoon, add the remaining marinated tomatoes. Discard any accumulated juices or the tomato juice will be too thin. Blend the combined tomatoes to make juice. Strain through a fine-mesh sieve. If not using right away, refrigerate the juice for up to 2 days.

GOOD MORNING VIETNAM

Amaro CioCiaro is rich in herbs and spices and carries a faint whiff of tobacco, cola, and cloves. The condensed coconut milk, which can be easily found online, gives this morning (or afternoon) cocktail a rich creaminess.

1½ ounces dark rum (such as Diplomático Reserva Exclusiva)

½ ounce Amaro CioCiaro

2 ounces cold-brew coffee

coconut cream, to taste (see recipe)

Serves 1

Combine the rum, Amaro CioCiaro, and cold-brew coffee in a Collins glass. Add ice, stir, and top with coconut cream.

WHAT YOU NEED TO KNOW

This recipe is easily increased to make a pitcher for brunch. Keep it chilled or use ice cubes made from coffee, so as not to dilute the flavor. Cold-brew coffee is sold bottled. If you can't source it, use cold espresso.

Coconut Cream Makes 1½ cups

1 cup condensed coconut milk

½ cup heavy cream

Combine.

Greg Bryson of the Wallace, Culver City

MORNING SEX

This is nearly as good as its namesake and best combined.

In an ice-filled cocktail shaker, combine the bourbon, passion fruit puree, lemon juice, chai syrup, and bitters and shake for about 20 seconds. Strain into ice-filled old-fashioned or Collins glasses or serve neat in chilled glasses.

8 ounces bourbon

4 ounces passion fruit puree (preferably Funkin or another brand that uses less than 10% sugar)

3 ounces freshly squeezed lemon juice

3 ounces chai syrup (see recipe)

1 teaspoon Peychaud's bitters

Makes 4 drinks

Chai Syrup Makes about ½ cup

6 tablespoons loose chai tea

½ cup water

½ cup sugar

Combine the tea mix with the water and sugar in a small saucepan. Bring to a boil, then lower the heat and simmer for 30 minutes. Strain, discarding the tea mix. Let cool to room temperature and then refrigerate for up to 5 days.

LIGHT FARE

Josiah Citrin of Charcoal, Venice Beach

CHARRED CUCUMBER GAZPACHO

Citrin intensifies the flavor of this gazpacho by charring half of the vegetables, lending them not only a smoky flavor but also a deliciously concentrated one. Smoked paprika further enhances the illusion of heat in this chilled soup.

CHARRED VEGETABLES

5 or 6 tomatoes, cut in half

2 Persian cucumbers

1 red bell pepper

2 tablespoons olive oil

2 teaspoons sel gris or fleur de sel

½ red onion, peeled and cut into ¼-inch slices

TO FINISH

5 or 6 ripe tomatoes, peeled, seeded, and cut into 8 pieces

1 Persian cucumber, peeled and coarsely chopped

½ red onion, peeled and coarsely chopped

1 stale piece sourdough bread

Serves 6

¼ cup Banyuls vinegar

1 garlic clove, minced

2 teaspoons smoked paprika

2 pinches of cayenne pepper

sel gris or fleur de sel

freshly ground black pepper

GARNISH

1 avocado, diced

fleur del sel

cracked black pepper

2 tablespoons finely chopped fresh chives

1 bunch basil, leaves picked and chopped fine

best olive oil, for drizzling

To make the charred vegetables, prepare a charcoal grill. Bank about two-thirds of the charcoal to one side of the grill; this will allow for two cooking zones.

Toss the tomatoes, cucumbers, and bell pepper with the olive oil and salt. Place them on the hotter side of the grill and cook, turning every 5 minutes or so, until charred black on all sides. Place the red onion slices on the cooler side of the grill and cook about 10 minutes on each side, until cooked through.

Remove the charred vegetables from the grill and let cool to room temperature. Peel and seed the bell pepper and cut into large chunks. Leave the charred skin on the tomatoes and cucumbers. Cut the tomatoes into eighths. Coarsely chop all but a few spoonfuls of the charred cucumber and all of the onion. Finely dice the remaining charred cucumber to use as a garnish.

To finish the gazpacho, combine both the charred and uncooked vegetables, the bread, vinegar, garlic, paprika, and cayenne in a blender or food processor and pulse until nearly smooth but still a bit chunky. Transfer to a bowl, season to taste with salt and ground pepper, and refrigerate until cold and for up to 12 hours.

Serve cold in chilled bowls. Garnish each serving with diced avocado and the reserved charred cucumber. Sprinkle with the fleur de sel, cracked pepper, chives, and basil. Drizzle with oil.

WHAT YOU NEED TO KNOW

Cutting the vegetables before putting them into the blender or food processor may sound unnecessary but it allows you to pulse the soup to a textured purée and not end up with any stray large chunks.

TOMATO SOUP

This is a forever recipe. Simple, silken, a modern rendition of an American classic, it's made luscious with extra-virgin olive oil instead of heavy cream.

10 big height-of-season beefsteak tomatoes or 15 plum tomatoes, cored and quartered	2 cups water
	2 cups good olive oil
	4 teaspoons sriracha
1 packed cup fresh basil leaves	1 tablespoon sugar
½ cup peeled garlic cloves	1 tablespoon kosher salt

Serves 6

Combine all of the ingredients in a large pot and simmer for 45 minutes. Whizz until smooth in a blender. Strain through a fine-mesh sieve and serve hot.

WHAT YOU NEED TO KNOW

The better your tomatoes, the better the soup. When blending hot liquids, it's best to do it in batches to avoid getting splattered and burned. A few thick slices of grilled bread brushed with olive oil and a well-dressed salad turns this soup into lunch or dinner.

Sara Kramer and Sarah Hymanson of Kismet, Los Feliz

CUCUMBER SALAD WITH ROSE LABNEH AND ZA'ATAR

This is a beautifully layered and nuanced salad of marinated cucumbers and cherries on a bed of labneh that's been scented with rose, sweetened with honey, and sharpened with garlic. A generous dusting of rose petal za'atar adds complexity. This one's far too gorgeous not to show off. Give it a final shower of dried rose petals and bring it to the table on a platter.

ROSE PETAL ZA'ATAR

⅓ cup dried rose petals

3 tablespoons tahini or freshly ground untoasted sesame seeds

1 tablespoon sesame seeds, toasted

2 teaspoons sumac

1 teaspoon salt

ROSE LABNEH

2½ cups whole Greek yogurt or labneh

1 to 1½ tablespoons honey

1 tablespoon rose water, or to taste

zest of 1 lemon, grated on a Microplane

½ garlic clove, grated on a Microplane

salt and freshly ground black pepper

CUCUMBER SALAD

1 cup cherries, pitted and halved

splash of red wine vinegar

1 teaspoon sugar

6 Persian cucumbers, peeled or not, as preferred

1 tablespoon olive oil

juice of 2 lemons

salt

1 handful fresh chervil or dill leaves

1 tablespoon dried rose petals

Serves 3 or 4 as an appetizer or 6 as a shared plate

To make the za'atar, stir the ingredients together until well-combined. Set aside in a sealed jar away from direct sunlight until ready to use.

To make the labneh, beat all of the ingredients together with a fork until well combined. Refrigerate, covered, until ready to use.

To make the cucumber salad, toss the cherries with the vinegar and sugar and set aside for half an hour or so.

Shave the cucumbers lengthwise on a mandoline. Toss the cucumbers with the oil and lemon juice and season with salt to taste. Set aside for half an hour or so.

To serve, spread the labneh on a platter. Drain the cucumbers, discarding the accumulated liquid, and drape the cucumber ribbons over the labneh. Drain the cherries, discarding the accumulated liquid, and scatter the cherries over the cucumbers. Sprinkle the salad generously with the za'atar and scatter with the chervil and the rose petals. Serve immediately.

WHAT YOU NEED TO KNOW

There are no tricks here, but try slicing the cucumbers lengthwise on a mandoline. They drape beautifully. Za'atar is wonderful on everything from roasted squash to flatbread. If time is short, use a store-bought za'atar and add dried rose petals. It's best to break up the petals a bit or give them a little rub between your palms to crumble them and release their aroma. Dean and DeLuca, Williams-Sonoma, and Jansal Valley all make excellent za'atar that is easily ordered online. The components of the salad may be made in advance, but do not assemble them until the last minute.

Jessica Koslow of Sqirl, Silver Lake

TOMATO SALAD WITH CRISPY POTATOES AND WHIPPED FETA

Good summer tomatoes seem even sweeter, juicier, and more pliant against the crunch of potato and the salinity of feta.

CRISPY POTATOES

1 pound baby potatoes (such as Peewee or fingerlings)

salt

½ cup olive oil, plus more as needed

WHIPPED FETA

7 ounces fresh feta (preferably sheep's milk), crumbled (about 1½ cups)

1 to 2 tablespoons 2% buttermilk, shaken

1½ teaspoons sumac

salt and pepper

TOMATOES

1¼ pounds heirloom tomatoes (red, yellow, green, or a mix), cored and cut into wedges or thick slices

small handful of very thinly-sliced red onion

1 tablespoon sherry vinegar

salt and pepper

TO FINISH

1 tablespoon fresh flat-leaf parsley leaves

1 tablespoon fresh chervil leaves

¼ cup fresh basil leaves

great olive oil, for drizzling

Serves 4

Preheat the oven to 425°F.

To make the crispy potatoes, scrub the potatoes and pat them dry, then heap them onto a rimmed baking sheet. Sprinkle with ½ teaspoon of salt and toss with the olive oil until evenly coated. Spread into a single layer and roast until crispy, 25 to 30 minutes, stirring every 10 minutes to make sure they're evenly browned.

Remove the potatoes from the oven. Roughly smash with a potato masher to flatten a bit, drizzle with more oil if needed, and lightly season with salt. Return to the oven and roast until browned and really crispy, another 20 to 25 minutes, turning them over halfway through the cooking time. Set aside to cool.

To make the whipped feta, in a food processor, blend the feta for 10 seconds to break it down. With the processor running, slowly pour in just enough buttermilk to make a sauce as thick and smooth as crème fraîche. If there are still lumps, scrape the sides and bottom of the processor with a rubber spatula and blend again until smooth. Blend in the sumac and season with salt and pepper to taste.

To make the tomatoes, in a large bowl, toss the tomatoes, red onion, and crispy potatoes (and any oil leftover from the sheet) with the vinegar, then season with salt and pepper to taste.

To serve, spread the whipped feta over a large serving platter and arrange the tomato and potato mixture on top. Sprinkle with the parsley, chervil, and basil and drizzle with olive oil.

WHAT YOU NEED TO KNOW

The potatoes here should be as crisp as croutons. If they're moist, let them bake longer. And, of course, use tomatoes at the height of their season. Tomatoes lose their flavor when refrigerated, so let them instead bask in the sun on a window ledge.

Josiah Citrin of Charcoal, Venice Beach

THREE SEASONS OF ARUGULA

Chef Citrin elevates basic arugula salads into seasonal, composed salads, balancing ripe fruit with tangy, salty feta and crunchy pumpkin seeds. Beautifully concocted vinaigrettes give the fruit a second dance, this time with the sweet, sour, and salty notes of vinegars, mustard, freshly squeezed citrus, and gray sea salt.

Toss the arugula and radicchio with the chosen vinaigrette. Assemble on four plates. Top with the feta, scatter with the pumpkin seeds, and add the fruit, per the recipes below.

WHAT YOU NEED TO KNOW

Consider the arugula salad a base recipe. The seasonal variations include additions—such as grilled peaches—and an aligned vinaigrette. Nothing here requires strict adherence to the rules. I love composed salads and often add additional seeds, grains, or nuts.

ARUGULA SALAD

4 cups arugula

1 head radicchio, torn into large pieces

¼ cup crumbled fresh feta cheese (preferably French)

2 tablespoons pumpkin seeds

approximately ⅓ cup chosen vinaigrette (recipes follow)

Serves 4

Grilled Peaches, Peach Vinaigrette Summer Variation

4 yellow peaches, ripe but firm

olive oil, as needed

salt

PEACH VINAIGRETTE

1 grilled peach (from above)

¼ cup freshly squeezed orange juice

1 tablespoon freshly squeezed lemon juice

¼ cup good sherry vinegar

2 tablespoons apple cider vinegar

1 tablespoon balsamic vinegar

1 tablespoon Dijon mustard

1 teaspoon sel gris or fleur de sel

1½ cups grapeseed oil

¾ cup olive oil

¼ cup pumpkin seed oil

To grill the peaches, prepare a charcoal or gas grill. Peel the peaches, halve them, and remove their pits. Cut each half into four wedges. Toss with olive oil and lightly season with salt. Grill on each side for 2 minutes, or until lightly colored. Set aside to cool.

To make the peach vinaigrette, transfer one of the peaches to a blender and puree until smooth. Pour the puree into a jar with a tight-fitting lid. Add the citrus juices, vinegars, mustard, and sel gris and shake well. Add the oils and shake again. If not using right away, refrigerate for up to 1 day and remove from the refrigerator 10 minutes before serving. Give the vinaigrette a last shaking right before dressing the salad.

Sliced Apple, Pumpkin Vinaigrette Fall Variation

1 Pink Lady apple, seeded, sliced thin on a mandolin

PUMPKIN VINAIGRETTE

1 small pumpkin or ½ cup pumpkin puree

¾ cup olive oil, plus more for the pumpkin

salt

freshly cracked black pepper

½ cup apple cider vinegar

¼ cup balsamic vinegar

juice of ½ lemon

1 tablespoon Dijon mustard

1 teaspoon sel gris or fleur de sel

½ shallot, finely diced

1 garlic clove, crushed into a paste

1½ cups grapeseed oil

¼ cup pumpkin seed oil

¼ cup water

If using a fresh pumpkin, preheat the oven to 350°F. Cut the pumpkin into small wedges. Toss with olive oil and lightly sprinkle with sea salt and cracked black pepper. Place on a baking sheet and bake until pumpkin is soft. The exact time will depend upon size. Set aside to cool.

Cut the skin off the pumpkin and discard. Transfer the flesh to a blender and puree until smooth.

To make the pumpkin vinaigrette, measure ½ cup of pumpkin puree and pour into a jar with a tight-fitting lid. Add the vinegars, lemon juice, mustard, sel gris, shallot, and garlic and shake well. Add the oils and shake again. If not using right away, refrigerate for up to 1 day and remove from the refrigerator 10 minutes before serving Give the vinaigrette a last shaking right before dressing the salad.

Blood Orange, Citrus Vinaigrette Winter Variation

1 blood orange, cut into segments

1 grapefruit, cut into segments

CITRUS VINAIGRETTE

½ cup freshly squeezed orange juice

¼ cup freshly squeezed grapefruit juice

2 tablespoons freshly squeezed lemon juice

2 tablespoons freshly squeezed lime juice

¼ cup simple syrup

¼ cup Champagne vinegar

1 teaspoon sel gris or fleur de sel

1½ cups grapeseed oil

¾ cup olive oil

¼ cup pumpkin seed oil

To make the citrus vinaigrette, combine the citrus juices, simple syrup, vinegar, and sel gris in a jar with a tight-fitting lid. Shake well. Add the oils and shake again. If not using right away, refrigerate for up to 1 day and and remove from the refrigerator 10 minutes before serving. Give the vinaigrette a last shaking right before dressing the salad.

CARAMELIZED CIPOLLINI ONION TARTE TATIN

Mozza is legendary for its mozzarella and pasta, but Silverton's menu holds other secrets. This tart is a particular favorite of mine. Silverton allows the sweetness of the cipollini onions to take center stage, only offset by a touch of thyme. Served with a salad, it makes for a lovely lunch or light supper.

1 pound cipollini onions, peeled and trimmed

salt and pepper

2 tablespoons butter, plus a bit more for brushing the puff pastry

2 tablespoons dark brown sugar

2 tablespoons fresh thyme leaves

1 sheet frozen puff pastry (about 14 ounces), thawed

Makes one 10-inch tart

Preheat the oven to 350°F. Cut the cipollini onions in half horizontally and season with salt and pepper.

Place the butter in an ovenproof 10- or 11-inch skillet and melt over medium heat. Once melted, tilt the skillet so that the butter evenly coats the bottom of the pan. Sprinkle the bottom of the pan with the brown sugar and thyme. Place the onions, cut side down, into the pan in a tightly packed single layer. Cook the onions until caramelized and fragrant, about 10 minutes. Remove from the heat.

Lay the puff pastry over the onions and trim any excess pastry that's hanging over the sides of the pan. Brush the top with melted butter and season with salt. Bake for 20 to 30 minutes, until the pastry is golden brown and the onions are tender. Let cool briefly before inverting onto a platter. Serve warm.

WHAT YOU NEED TO KNOW

Cipollini are small, flat, pale onions, with a delicate flavor and a thin, papery skin. They're most often available in the autumn. I use frozen puff pastry for this recipe. My brand of choice is Dufour, which comes in 14-ounce packages and is widely available in gourmet shops.

While it is easiest to make a single, large tart, you may also make individual tarts. Simply cut circles of the pastry to lay over each onion. Bake, as directed.

AVOCADO HUMMUS WITH FRESH ZA'ATAR SALAD

This is, to me, the taste of Los Angeles today: homegrown avocados spun into a luscious green hummus and topped with a fresh za'atar salad. Serve with toasted or grilled pita.

HUMMUS

1 cup cooked chickpeas

2 tablespoons tahini

¼ cup freshly squeezed lemon juice

¼ cup olive oil, plus a bit more as needed

3 garlic cloves, chopped

½ teaspoon kosher salt

4 ripe Hass avocados, peeled and pitted

ZA'ATAR SALAD

4 cups fresh flat-leaf parsley leaves

a few stems of thyme, leaves picked

1 tablespoon sesame seeds, toasted

2 teaspoons sumac

2 tablespoons olive oil

2 tablespoons freshly squeezed lemon juice

salt and pepper

maldon sea salt, for serving

warmed, grilled, or toasted pita, for serving

To make the hummus, combine the chickpeas, tahini, lemon juice, olive oil, garlic, and salt in a food processor and process until the mixture is perfectly smooth. Add the avocados and process again until smooth. Scrape the sides and the bottom of the processor with a rubber spatula, give the processor another quick spin, and taste the hummus for seasoning.

To make the za'atar salad, toss all of the ingredients in a mixing bowl. It should be fairly dry, not overdressed. Season to taste.

To serve, top the hummus with the za'atar salad. Sprinkle with the Maldon sea salt and serve with pita.

Serves 6 as an appetizer or shared plate

Conor Shemtov of Mh Zh, Silver Lake

HUMMUS BLING BLING

Odd as it may sound, there's something romantic about this hummus. You will fall in love with it. Topped with toasted pine nuts, a shower of minced parsley, a swirl of deeply browned nutty butter, and best of all, a scattering of caraway-infused pickled raisins, this demands a spoon, not just a wedge of store-bought pita. It demands candlelight and thick slices of olive oil–brushed grilled bread. It demands a moment after each bite to savor the mingling of textures and flavors.

Mh Zh is short for the Hebrew *mah zeh*, which translates roughly as "what's that," but, in popular parlance, is an intensifier, suggesting that something inspires awe, and chef-owner Shemtov's outdoor café does exactly that.

HUMMUS

8 ounces dried chickpeas

2 teaspoons baking soda

½ cup olive oil, plus a bit more as needed

⅓ cup tahini

juice of 1 lemon, plus a bit more as needed

2 garlic cloves, minced

1 teaspoon salt

¼ to ½ cup ice water

PICKLED GOLDEN RAISINS

1 teaspoon caraway seeds

½ cup golden raisins

½ cup apple cider or distilled white vinegar

¼ cup water

2 garlic cloves, thinly sliced

salt

BROWN BUTTER

1 tablespoon nonfat dry milk powder (optional)

½ cup butter

TO SERVE

2 tablespoons minced fresh flat-leaf parsley

½ cup pine nuts, toasted until pale gold

grilled bread or pita brushed with olive oil

Serves 6 as an appetizer or shared plate

To make the hummus, place the chickpeas in a large bowl with 1 teaspoon of the baking soda. Add enough cold water to cover by at least 3 inches. Let these soak overnight.

The following day, drain the chickpeas and transfer them to a stockpot. Fill with 3 quarts of water and the remaining 1 teaspoon baking soda. Bring to a boil and skim off the foam. Lower the heat and simmer until very tender, as in melt-in-your-mouth tender, about 2 hours. Remove from the heat and let the chickpeas cool in their cooking liquid. Once cool enough to handle, peel the chickpeas.

Combine the olive oil, tahini, lemon juice, garlic, and salt in a food processor and process until well blended. Add 2 tablespoons of the ice water and process again. Add 3 cups of the cooked chickpeas and continue to process. With the processor running, add as much of the remaining water in a thin stream as you need to lighten the consistency to your liking. The hummus will be ready when it is entirely smooth and light in texture, somewhat like fresh ice cream. Taste and add more olive oil and lemon juice, if needed. If not serving right away, keep refrigerated for up to 2 days.

To make the pickled raisins, toast the caraway seeds in a dry frying pan over medium heat until fragrant, 2 to 3 minutes. Place the raisins in a small bowl. Combine the vinegar, water, toasted caraway seeds, garlic, and a good pinch of salt in a saucepan and bring to a boil. Lower the heat and simmer for a few minutes to warm through and then pour over the raisins. Let steep for 30 minutes, then drain, discarding the pickling liquid.

To make the brown butter, grind the milk powder, if using, into oblivion using a coffee grinder. Set aside. In a wide saucepan, melt the butter over medium heat. Once it has melted, whisk in the milk powder until no lumps remain. Turn the heat to low and continue whisking while the butter browns. The mixture will foam and can darken quickly. Keep a weather eye on it and remove it from the heat as soon as it reaches a golden brown.

Twenty minutes before you plan to serve the hummus, remove it from the fridge. After 20 minutes, it should be cool, but not cold. Spoon the hummus into a shallow serving bowl, scatter with the parsley, pine nuts, and raisins, and drizzle with the brown butter. Serve with grilled bread or pita.

WHAT YOU NEED TO KNOW

Tahini separates when stored, and a layer of oil forms on top. Discard this oil and simply add more olive oil, if needed. The trick to making hummus is to have more of all of the ingredients on hand—more tahini, olive oil, lemon juice, garlic, salt, ice water—and adjust to your satisfaction.

If you can bear doing it, skinning the cooked chickpeas will make the hummus billowy, even cloudlike. To skin a cooked chickpea, press it between your thumb and first two fingers. If needed, give a little rub. The chickpea should pop out of its skin.

Shemtov adds milk powder when browning his butter because the added sugar and proteins increase the yield of dark golden flecks. But this step is entirely optional, and the butter will still be just as deliciously nutty without it.

Mh Zh

I fell hard for this corner spot in Sunset Junction with nary an inside table nor a sign on the door, only some outdoor metal chairs, tables, and a daily menu scrawled in Sharpie on a brown paper-bag. A place, in short, that is all about the food, and the food happens to be outstanding. Chef-owner Conor Shemtov looks even younger than his 27 years and is quick to credit his Israeli grandmother with many of his recipes, but his knowledge of Mediterranean cooking belies his boyish humility. Get him talking about cooking, and an encyclopedic wealth of information pours out of him with a charmingly unselfconscious charisma. His food, however, is already the stuff of a master.

LE PUY LENTILS WITH SALSA VERDE

Fennel seeds, cocktail onions, and preserved lemons give this salsa verde both dimension and surprise. It brightens the earthiness of the lentils and offers the freshness a dried legume demands. I love this dish in a bowl for lunch, perhaps topped with a poached egg, but save some for a dinner of seared salmon or trout.

LENTILS

olive oil, as needed

1 yellow onion, halved

1 celery stalk, trimmed and cut in half

1 carrot, peeled and cut in half

1 head of garlic, halved crosswise

2 tablespoons kosher salt

1 Fresno chile, halved lengthwise

1 cup dry white wine

2 cups French lentils (preferably Le Puy)

VINAIGRETTE

½ shallot, chopped

½ cup red wine vinegar

1 cup olive oil

salt

SALSA VERDE

1 packed cup chopped fresh flat-leaf parsley

1 large garlic clove, grated on a Microplane or minced

2 anchovy fillets packed in oil, chopped

1 teaspoon finely chopped preserved lemon

1 teaspoon chopped, jarred, pickled cocktail onions

1 teaspoon capers, coarsely chopped

1½ teaspoons freshly squeezed lemon juice

1 teaspoon red wine vinegar

2 teaspoons fennel seeds, toasted and ground

pinch of kosher salt

5 turns of freshly cracked black pepper

¼ cup olive oil

2 tablespoons water

TO SERVE

handful of chopped parsley

spoonful of minced shallots

1 Fresno chile, chopped

maldon sea salt

freshly ground black pepper

juice of 1 lemon (optional)

Serves 6

To make the lentils, heat a saucepot over high heat. Pour in enough olive oil to lightly coat the bottom of the pot, then add the onion, celery, carrot, garlic, salt and chile. Sear the vegetables until they've started to char. Add the wine and cook until reduced by about three-fourths. Add the lentils to the pot and pour in enough water to cover them by 3 inches. Bring to a boil, then lower the heat and simmer, stirring occasionally, until the lentils are cooked through but still offer a bit of bite, 20 to 25 minutes. Your aim is to pull them off heat about 5 minutes before they are tender. Let the lentils cool in their cooking liquid to room temperature, then drain. Or, if not using right away, refrigerate the lentils in their cooking liquid, then drain before using them.

To make the vinaigrette, combine the shallot and vinegar in a mixing bowl and let sit for 10 minutes. While whisking, pour in the olive oil. Season with a touch of salt and set aside.

To make the salsa verde, combine all of the ingredients in a mixing bowl and stir until combined, pressing lightly on the anchovies with the back of the spoon to help incorporate them into the oil. Refrigerate until needed, but not longer than 24 hours or the parsley will lose its vibrancy and the garlic will grow too pungent.

To serve, bring the drained lentils to room temperature, if they've been chilled, and toss in a bowl with parsley, shallots, and chile. Season with salt and pepper. Dress and toss with the vinaigrette until lightly coated. Squeeze the lemon over the lentils, if you want a bit of pucker. Serve each portion with a generous dollop of the salsa verde.

WHAT YOU NEED TO KNOW

Splurge, if you can, on French Le Puy lentils or Castelluccio lentils from the Umbrian region of Italy. Both hold their shape when cooked, which is not necessarily true for all lentils. Leftover salsa verde is good on everything from grilled fish to tomato salad.

BEEF TONNATO

I may have had one too many tuna sandwiches in cafeterias to ever willingly eat another, but I will eat a good tonnato sauce by the spoonful. I'll happily lather it onto grilled bread, smear it onto veal, pork, beef, or poached chicken and dollop it generously onto grilled peppers with ready pleasure. Chef Pollack makes his version of the classic Italian vitello tonnato with roast beef, not veal.

BEEF

1½ pounds beef, either eye of round or tenderloin

salt and pepper

2 teaspoons vegetable or grapeseed oil

TONNATO SAUCE

1 (5-ounce) can tuna packed in oil, drained

⅔ cup mayonnaise, store-bought or homemade (see recipe)

3 tablespoons anchovy fillets packed in oil, coarsely chopped

1 tablespoon capers

1 tablespoon coarsely chopped shallots

2 or 3 garlic cloves, coarsely chopped

5 teaspoons freshly squeezed lemon juice

2 tablespoons Dijon mustard

1 tablespoon white wine vinegar

freshly ground black pepper

TO SERVE

2 hard-boiled eggs, yolks only

1 to 2 lemons, halved

3 tablespoons olive oil

freshly ground black pepper

½ cup celery leaves

15 caper berries

1 loosely packed cup bonito flakes

Serves 4

If you are dry-brining the beef, generously season it with salt and pepper and refrigerate, wrapped in plastic wrap, for 8 to 24 hours.

About an hour before you plan to roast the beef, remove it from the fridge and preheat the oven to 250°F. (If you have not dry-brined it, generously season it with salt and pepper at this time.)

Unwrap the beef, pat it dry, and place it in a roasting pan. Roast the beef until it reaches 127°F. Start checking for doneness after 1 hour; depending upon the thickness, it may take up to 90 minutes. Remove the beef from the oven and let rest at room temperature for 1 hour. Wrap it in aluminum foil and refrigerate for at least 4 hours and up to 8 hours.

Remove the beef from the fridge, unwrap it, and pat it dry with paper towels. Heat a cast-iron or other heavy skillet over high heat until it is extremely hot. Pour in the oil, give it a quick swirl, and sear the beef on all sides until it has formed a nice brown crust. Return the beef to the fridge for 1 to 2 hours to cool once more.

To make the tonnato sauce, place the tuna, mayonnaise, anchovy, capers, shallots, garlic, lemon juice, mustard, and vinegar in a food processor, season with the pepper, and process until homogenous. Zach likes to retain a bit of chunkiness; I like it silky smooth.

To serve, put your serving plates in the fridge to chill. Pass the hard-boiled egg yolks through a fine-mesh sieve and set aside. Carve the beef into very thin slices, not more than ¼-inch thick.

Spread the tonnato sauce over the bottom of the cold plates, coming to within about an inch of the edge. Drape the slices of beef over the tonnato, creasing it in places so it creates a wavy pattern of beef with nooks and crannies. Squeeze a bit of lemon juice over the top, drizzle with the olive oil, and season with a few grinds of black pepper. Garnish with the celery leaves, the sieved egg yolk, caper berries and bonito flakes and serve.

WHAT YOU NEED TO KNOW

Tonnato sauce makes a mean sandwich—try it with leftover roasted beef or pork, a handful of arugula, and thick slices of bread brushed with olive oil and almost charred over a flame. This dish is traditionally served as an appetizer, but I think of it as a light meal on a warm day. Nothing more than a salad is needed, except maybe some bread to scoop up the last of the tonnato. If you have the time to dry-brine the beef a day in advance, it will be that much more flavorful. But this step is not essential, as the recipe has umami to spare.

Homemade Mayonnaise Makes a little more than 1 cup

This is my quick go-to blender recipe. If your blender is particularly wide, you'll need to use a small mixing bowl and electric beaters, an immersion blender, or a good old whisk instead. Or, even better, double the recipe and use leftovers for sandwiches. Homemade mayonnaise should last in a sealed jar for 5 days.

Should you wish, add a minced clove or two of garlic, a pinch of saffron, a teaspoon of Dijon mustard, a pinch of smoked paprika or any other manner of flavor or spice that does not add to the liquidity. Do this before adding the oil. With the addition of mustard, you may want to cut the salt back to ¼ teaspoon.

1 egg

1 tablespoon freshly squeezed lemon juice

½ teaspoon salt

a few grindings of white pepper (optional)

1 cup olive oil, or a combination of olive oil and grapeseed, canola, or vegetable

Place the egg, lemon juice, salt, and white pepper, if using, in a blender and quickly pulse. With the blender running, very, very slowly pour in the oil in a thin, steady stream. Continue to blend until the mixture looks like mayonnaise.

David LeFevre of Manhattan Beach Post, Manhattan Beach

POMEGRANATE COUSCOUS

Ruby-red pomegranate arils, salty, tangy feta, puckering grapefruit, and oily Marcona almonds give basic couscous layers of texture, flavor, and color. It's a light lunch, an appetizer, picnic food, or a side dish served on a warm night with grilled meat or fish.

COUSCOUS

1½ cups Moroccan couscous

1 tablespoon olive oil

2¼ cups vegetable or chicken stock

2 tablespoons minced red onion

1 garlic clove, minced

¼ teaspoon ground turmeric

salt and pepper

½ cup finely diced cucumber

¼ cup finely chopped fresh mint

¼ cup finely chopped fresh cilantro

VINAIGRETTE

2 tablespoons red wine vinegar

1 tablespoon honey

1 tablespoon Dijon mustard

6 tablespoons olive oil

salt and pepper

TO SERVE

¾ cup pomegranate arils

½ cup Marcona almonds

1 pound, 2 ounces fresh feta cheese (preferably French), crumbled

1 Ruby Red grapefruit, cut into segments, then cut into thirds

1 lemon, halved

½ cup whole milk Greek yogurt (optional)

To make the couscous, combine the couscous and olive oil in a mixing bowl and stir to coat. In a small saucepot, combine the stock, onion, garlic, and turmeric and season with salt and pepper. Bring to a boil, then remove from the heat.

Pour the hot stock over the couscous and cover tightly with plastic wrap. Set aside in a warm place to steam for 10 minutes. Remove the plastic wrap and fluff the couscous with a fork. Gently toss with the cucumber, mint, and cilantro.

To make the vinaigrette, whisk the vinegar, honey, and mustard together in a small bowl. Continuing to whisk, pour in the olive oil. Season with salt and pepper to taste and set aside.

To serve, toss the couscous with the vinaigrette in a large serving bowl. Sprinkle the pomegranate seeds, almonds, feta and grapefruit over the top. Squeeze the lemon over it all. Serve with a dollop of yogurt.

WHAT YOU NEED TO KNOW

This recipe also works well with Israeli couscous, farro, fregola, barley, freekeh or most any small grain. Adjust the cooking instructions according to your choice of grain. You may toast the grains if that's your preference.

Serves 4 for lunch or 6 as a side dish

Jaime Martin del Campo and Ramiro Arvizu of La Casita Mexicana, Bell

QUESO FUNDIDO A LAS FINAS HIERBAS

Fresh herbs and a nuanced assortment of Mexican cheeses make this queso fundido particularly good.

1 teaspoon butter

1 teaspoon thinly sliced jalapeño chile

¾ cup grated Oaxaca cheese

¾ cup grated queso panela

¾ cup grated queso fresco

¼ cup grated Cotija cheese

2 tablespoons crema Mexicana

1 teaspoon chopped fresh cilantro

1 teaspoon chopped fresh parsley

1 teaspoon chopped fresh epazote

1 teaspoon chopped fresh hoja santa

4 tortillas, warmed, for serving

Serves 2 to 4

Preheat the oven to 350°F.

Heat a frying pan over medium heat. Add the butter and the jalapeño and cook for 2 minutes.

In a mixing bowl, combine the cheeses, crema Mexicana, and herbs. Add the jalapeño and the butter in which it was cooked and stir thoroughly.

Transfer the mixture to a cast-iron skillet or gratin dish and bake for 5 minutes. Stir and return to the oven to bake for an additional 5 minutes or until the cheese has melted and is bubbling.

Serve with warm tortillas.

WHAT YOU NEED TO KNOW

This is all about the shopping, but there are a few possible substitutions. If you don't have queso fresco on hand, a plain, young chèvre may be used or even a mild feta. It's easier to grate cheeses when they are cold, but crumbling them is just fine. Hoja santa may be hard to find. It's also called Mexican pepperleaf or root beer plant. If you can't find it, simply double the amount of epazote. And if you can't find epazote, simply double the amount of fresh cilantro. You'll want to serve this with tortillas that have been warmed but not crisped.

SESAME NORI–CRUSTED KANPACHI

This dish sounds mild, what with flowers and plums and a passion fruit vinaigrette. But don't let that fool you. The serrano keeps it sharp, while the aonori brings you the brine of the Pacific.

1 tablespoon avocado oil, grapeseed oil or olive oil

1 pluot, plum, or other stone fruit, stone removed, cut into 8 wedges

kosher salt

1 lemon, halved

1 passion fruit

2 nasturtiums or other edible flowers, minced

olive oil, as needed

1 small serrano chile, seeded and cut into paper-thin slices (optional)

1 tablespoon toasted sesame seeds

1 tablespoon aonori (see note)

maldon sea salt

7 ounces sashimi-grade kanpachi or yellowtail, cleaned and trimmed by a fishmonger

———

Serves 2

Heat the avocado oil in a small skillet over medium-high heat. When the oil is hot and shimmering, carefully add the pluot wedges and sear until caramelized on both sides, 2 to 3 minutes. Sprinkle with a pinch of kosher salt and squeeze a bit of lemon juice over the top. Set aside to cool.

While the pluots cool, halve the passion fruit and scoop the pulp into a small bowl. Add the flowers and whisk in 1 tablespoon olive oil. Season with a pinch of kosher salt and a couple of drops of lemon juice. Stir in the serrano chile slices, if using, and set aside.

Combine the sesame seeds, aonori, and a pinch of Maldon sea salt. Spread the sesame seed mixture in a single layer on a plate.

Rub the kanpachi with a thin smear of olive oil on one side and coat it with the sesame seed mixture by placing it directly on the seeds and pressing down ever so gently.

Heat a skillet over medium-high heat until hot. With tongs and a paper towel, lightly coat the bottom of the pan with olive oil. Sear the fish on the sesame seed-coated side only until lightly browned, 10 to 20 seconds. Set aside to cool.

When cool, cut the kanpachi against the grain into ¼-inch slices. Divide the fish slices between two plates in a pretty, scattered pattern, alternating with the pluot wedges. Season with a little Maldon sea salt and a few drops of lemon juice. Drizzle with the passion fruit vinaigrette and serve immediately.

WHAT YOU NEED TO KNOW

Kanpachi is a yellowtail fish, native to the Pacific, and often used in Japan for sushi and sashimi. Another sashimi-grade yellowtail may be substituted. Aonori, ground dried seaweed, is easily found online.

ORSA & WINSTON

What with four restaurants in the space of a few blocks, Josef Centeno might well be called the culinary mayor of DTLA (downtown Los Angeles). Before DTLA became a destination for art and food lovers, it was an urban wasteland. Centeno's first restaurant, Bäco Mercat did for the neighborhood what the Odeon did for Tribeca in New York when it opened in 1980—it created a buzzing hub for the locals, making up for the lack of grocery stores and public transportation. And who really needs groceries when Centeno now has most every hankering covered? In Bar Amá, he conjures the Tejano cooking of his childhood; in Bäco Mercat, he delivers bold Mediterranean fare; P.Y.T. is best described as a love song to a nearby garden; and Orsa & Winston is an ambitious, highly personal tour de force in Japanese and Italian gastronomy.

TUNA CRUDO PUTTANESCA

Here, chef Hopson uses fresh tuna in place of canned anchovies to give a classic Italian sauce a fresh Californian spin. Without the pasta and the tomatoes, there's nothing separating you from the fiery fury of this fantastic raw dish.

PUTTANESCA

small bunch of flat-leaf parsley, leaves picked

10 oil-cured, pitted black olives

1 shallot

3 tablespoons capers

⅓ cup olive oil

CALABRIAN CHILE–FENNEL CONFIT

½ large fennel bulb or 2 small wild fennel bulbs, sliced thin

¾ cup plus 2 tablespoons olive oil

2 teaspoons to 1½ tablespoons Calabrian chiles packed in oil, minced

2 pounds sushi-grade tuna loin, skin removed

maldon sea salt

Serves 6

To make the puttanesca, mince the parsley, olives, shallot, and capers and combine thoroughly in a bowl. Stir in the olive oil.

To make the Calabrian chile–fennel confit, preheat the oven to 250°F. Toss the fennel with the olive oil in a small lidded pot and cover. Bake for 45 minutes to 1 hour, or until the fennel has been cooked through but hasn't turned to mush. Let the fennel cool in the oil, then remove it and mince it.

Stir together the fennel confit and Calabrian chile.

Slice the tuna into ⅜-inch slices. The slices should be thin but not so thin that you lose the texture of the fish.

Fan the tuna on a platter or plates and top with the puttanesca. Serve with a dollop of fennel confit and a light sprinkle of Maldon sea salt.

WHAT YOU NEED TO KNOW

Bottled Calabrian chiles in oil are available at specialty grocery stores, Italian food shops, and online. They are spicy, so add accordingly. The Calabrian chile–fennel confit may be made ahead and stored in the fridge for up to five days.

SWEET POTATOES, TAHINI, GREENS, AND HARISSA VINAIGRETTE

The haunting voice of the high priestess of soul, Nina Simone, inspired Largey to name her first restaurant after her first musical love. Simone fits right into the revival of the Downtown Arts District. It's seasonal, casual, and offers a roof garden and an on-site butchery. Sit at the chef's counter for a tasting menu or graze on local greens at a table. This layered dish has so many disparate textures and flavors that I defy even the staunchest carnivore to resist it.

SWEET POTATOES

2 large sweet potatoes

a few spoonfuls of coconut oil

maldon sea salt

SHISHITO PEPPERS

12 to 16 shishito peppers

a few teaspoons of grapeseed oil

salt

juice of 1 lime

HARISSA VINAIGRETTE

2 shallots, finely diced

olive oil, as needed

1 tablespoon harissa

1 tablespoon Champagne vinegar

juice of ½ lemon

salt and pepper

TAHINI SAUCE

½ cup tahini (preferably Soom brand)

1 tablespoon white miso

1 tablespoon toasted sesame oil

juice of ½ lemon

3 to 4 tablespoons water, at room temperature

maldon sea salt

TO SERVE

2 tangerines or 1 orange, cut into segments

1 bunch of mustard greens, picked, washed, and dried

a few nasturtiums (optional), for garnish

Serves 2

WHAT YOU NEED TO KNOW

If shishito peppers are out of season, substitute snap peas. Likewise, arugula can be swapped in for the mustard greens, as can oranges for the tangerines, and butternut squash for the sweet potatoes. An edible flower adds a pretty flourish here: nasturtium, pea, chive, or cilantro flowers all fit the bill.

Preheat the oven to 400°F.

To make the sweet potatoes, peel them and cut into 2-inch pieces. Melt a few spoonfuls of coconut oil in a pan over low heat or set the pan in a warm place near the oven. Toss the sweet potatoes with the melted coconut oil and season with salt. Spread the chunks onto a baking sheet and roast for 20 minutes. Remove the sweet potatoes from the oven, give them a toss, and roast for another 5 or 10 minutes, or until tender inside and crispy outside.

To make the shishito peppers, clean them, remove the tops, and pat them dry with paper towels. Heat a lidded skillet over high heat and add the grapeseed oil. Add the shishitos and cook, tossing so that they cook evenly. Once they start to blister, turn the heat to medium and partially cover with a lid. Once cooked to your liking, remove from the heat and season with salt and lime juice to taste.

To make the harissa vinaigrette, put the shallots in a small saucepan and add just enough olive oil to cover. Stir in the harissa and heat over low heat until the shallots become translucent. Remove from the heat and stir in the Champagne vinegar and lemon juice. Season to taste.

To make the tahini sauce, whisk together the tahini, miso, sesame oil, lemon juice, and 3 tablespoons of the water in a bowl. The sauce will emulsify as you continue to whisk. If you find the tahini too thick, add another tablespoon of water. Season with salt to taste.

To serve, spread the tahini sauce abundantly on two plates or a platter. Top with the roasted sweet potatoes, followed by the shishito peppers and the citrus segments. Drizzle with a bit of the vinaigrette. In a separate bowl, toss the greens with vinaigrette. Top the potatoes with the dressed greens. Sprinkle with nasturtiums.

CHICKEN SALAD WITH INDIAN SPICES

Chef Silverton likes the food on her plate to look like it either fell from the sky or grew from the plate. I like to imagine the Little Gem lettuces and slivers of preserved lemon in this salad floating down to my plate from a big, bountiful, and billowy cloud. In this lovely dish, the chicken is scented with Indian spices and then cooked, shredded, and tossed with a lemon vinaigrette, tender greens, and toasted walnuts. Simple, but the spice mixture will have you returning to this recipe again and again.

SPICE MIX

1 chile de arbol

1 cinnamon stick

2 bay leaves

¼ cup cumin seeds

¼ cup coriander seeds

1 tablespoon green cardamom pods

1 tablespoon peppercorns

2 teaspoons whole cloves

1 teaspoon ground turmeric

1 teaspoon fenugreek

½ teaspoon ground nutmeg

CHICKEN

8 chicken breasts, bone-in, skin-on

salt

olive oil

VINAIGRETTE

¼ cup minced shallots

¼ cup freshly squeezed lemon juice

1 tablespoon Champagne vinegar

1 teaspoon kosher salt

½ cup olive oil

½ teaspoon freshly ground black pepper

SALAD

a few heads Little Gem lettuces, leaves separated, washed and dried

1 or 2 heads escarole

¼ preserved lemon rind, slivered

1 cup fresh cilantro leaves (preferably micro cilantro)

1 cup walnuts, toasted and coarsely chopped

pinch of red pepper flakes

maldon sea salt

freshly cracked black pepper

Serves 8

To make the spice mix, grind all of the ingredients to a powder in a Vitamix or a spice grinder or coffee grinder.

To make the chicken, season the chicken breasts with salt and then rub generously with the ground spice mix, making sure to cover the meat under the skin. Refrigerate for at least 2 hours and up to 24 hours.

Remove the chicken from the fridge half an hour before cooking to let it come to room temperature. Brush off any remaining salt and spice. Preheat the broiler and set a rack so that the chicken is at least 6 inches from the heat source. (If your rack is not adjustable, roast the chicken instead at 425°F.)

To broil the chicken, rub the chicken breasts in olive oil and place them on a broiler pan skin side down. Broil for 15 minutes, then flip and broil another 10 minutes, or until the juices run clear. The timing will depend upon the size of the chicken breasts and their proximity to the heat source. Let the chicken cool.

When the chicken is cool enough to handle, shred or chop it into pieces. Discard the skin and bones.

To make the vinaigrette, combine the shallots, lemon juice, vinegar, and salt in a small bowl and let sit for 10 minutes. While whisking, pour in the oil in a slow, steady stream. Whisk in the ground pepper.

To assemble the salad, toss all of the salad ingredients together in a big bowl and season with Maldon salt and cracked pepper to taste. Add the vinaigrette and toss to coat. Top with the chicken and drizzle with a bit more of the vinaigrette.

WHAT YOU NEED TO KNOW

Silverton cooks the chicken sous vide at Mozza, but at home, it can be broiled, roasted, or grilled. Likewise, I've used this spice mix on a whole chicken and roasted it, serving it with the salad and couscous on the side; you could also shred it and add it directly to the salad.

Phuong Tran of Croft Alley, West Hollywood

TURKEY BANH MI

Born in Vietnam, raised in New Orleans, and trained by Thomas Keller and Jean-Georges Vongerichten, Tran brings a simple grace and a light touch to this classic sandwich in a secret hideaway off Melrose Place.

PICKLED CARROT AND DAIKON

1 carrot, peeled and julienned

1 daikon, peeled and julienned

4 cups rice wine vinegar

¼ cup sugar

TURKEY SLIDERS

2 jalapeño chiles

2 scallions

2 pounds ground turkey

2 tablespoons finely grated fresh ginger

1 tablespoon finely grated garlic

1½ tablespoons fish sauce

1 teaspoon sugar

grapeseed oil, for frying

TO SERVE

2 baguettes

aioli or mayonnaise, for spreading

sriracha

1 bunch cilantro, leaves picked

2 Fresno chiles, sliced

1 English cucumber, sliced thin

Makes 6 sandwiches

To make the pickled carrot and daikon, combine all of the ingredients in a medium bowl and let sit for at least 30 minutes and up to 2 hours. Drain.

To make the sliders, core, seed, and thinly slice the jalapeños. Thinly slice the white and pale green parts of the scallions. In a large mixing bowl, combine all of the ingredients except the oil. Use your hands to mix thoroughly, really working it all together. Shape the turkey mixture into 24 patties.

Line a plate with paper towels. In a sauté pan, pour in enough grapeseed oil to lightly coat the bottom of the pan and set over medium heat. Add the sliders in batches, so as not to overcrowd the pan, and cook about 6 minutes on each side, or until to your liking. Transfer to the paper towel–lined plate.

To assemble the sandwiches, cut the baguettes so that you have six pieces, each around 6 inches long. Slice horizontally and toast if so desired. Spread the aioli on both sides of the baguette , and give them a little squirt of sriracha. Line the bottom of each baguette with sliders, a few sprigs of cilantro, a sprinkle of Fresno chiles, some sliced cucumber, and the pickled carrots and daikon. Serve with plenty of napkins.

Emily Fiffer and Heather Sperling of Botanica, Silver Lake

ROMESCO, COMPOSED OR DEVOURED SOLO

This is hands down the best romesco I've ever had. A Spanish dish that falls somewhere between a sauce, a dip, and the star of a meal, romesco is as thick as hummus, as textured as pesto, and as vivid as a Rothko. In Spain, it's traditionally served with grilled seafood. Here, Fiffer and Sperling let it take center stage, pairing it with charred peppers, crisped potatoes, seared leeks, a garland of grilled broccolini and a fluttering of cilantro flowers. It couldn't be prettier. But it's also delicious lavished on a thick slice of grilled bread that's been brushed with good olive oil and rubbed with a clove of garlic.

ROMESCO

4 red bell peppers

1 cup toasted blanched almonds

¼ cup chopped fresh cilantro

1 jalapeño chile, seeded

2 garlic cloves

¼ cup olive oil

1 tablespoon good sherry vinegar

zest and juice of 1 small lemon

2 teaspoons Spanish smoked paprika

salt

TO SERVE

20 tiny potatoes, boiled in salted water until just tender

excellent olive oil, as needed

flaky sea salt and pepper

Spanish smoked paprika, for sprinkling

3 or 4 small leeks, white and light green parts only, halved lengthwise

12 shishito peppers

2 or 3 bunches broccolini

zest and juice of 2 lemons, to taste

cilantro flowers, micro cilantro, or fresh cilantro leaves

———

Serves 4

To make the romesco, preheat the oven to 450°F and roast the bell peppers until blistered and soft. Transfer the peppers to a bowl or, even better, a paper bag, cover, and let sit for 10 minutes. Once cool enough to handle, remove the seeds and stems and whatever skin can easily be peeled away, working over a bowl to catch all of the good juices.

In a food processor, combine the roasted peppers with the remaining ingredients, plus a splash of liquid from the peppers. Process until fully incorporated, but not fully uniform; some texture is ideal here. Taste and add more almonds, cilantro, olive oil, vinegar, and salt, as needed; the romesco should be smoky, savory, and punchily acidic.

Use immediately or store in a sealed jar in the fridge for up to 1 day. After 1 day, the romesco will still be good, if given a stir, but the garlic will be more pungent.

Lightly crush each boiled potato with the side of a knife. Pour in enough olive oil to lightly coat the bottom of a frying pan and set over medium heat. Add the potatoes and sauté until the bottoms are just starting to crisp, then flip and crisp up the other side. Transfer to a paper towel-lined plate with a slotted spoon, season well with salt, pepper, and a sprinkle of paprika.

While the potatoes are crisping, prepare a grill or heat a large skillet over high heat. If using a skillet, pour in enough olive oil to lightly coat the bottom of the pan. Cook the leeks, cut side down, until they start to caramelize, then flip them and cook for a few minutes on the other side, until softened throughout. Repeat with the shishito peppers.

Toss the broccolini with enough olive oil to lightly coat and season with salt and pepper. Either grill or sear them in the skillet until al dente and lightly charred.

To serve, mound the romesco in the center of the dish and place the potatoes, leeks, peppers and broccolini in a ring around the perimeter so that they look like a vegetable garland or crown. Finish with a squeeze of lemon juice, a good drizzle of excellent olive oil, lots of lemon zest, a sprinkle of flaky sea salt, and lots and lots of cilantro flowers.

WHAT YOU NEED TO KNOW

The quantity of almonds may be increased to make the romesco milder.

SEARED JAPANESE SWEET POTATOES WITH SALSA VERDE

This recipe represents everything that I love about Botanica—boldly seasoned, healthy ingredients and gorgeous presentation. The Japanese sweet potatoes will have a custard-like interior beneath a crisp skin. The piquant salsa verde will offset the sweetness, and the lemon will wake it all up.

SALSA VERDE

2 large shallots, minced

2 tablespoons sherry vinegar

2 bunches parsley, finely chopped (tender stems are okay, too!)

2 bunches cilantro, finely chopped (ditto)

¼ cup capers, coarsely chopped

2 large garlic cloves, minced

juice of 2 lemons

2 cups California olive oil

salt and pepper

SWEET POTATOES

16 Japanese sweet potatoes

olive oil, as needed

TO SERVE

salt and pepper

zest of 1 lemon

Serves 8

To make the salsa verde, place the shallots and sherry vinegar in a medium jar, stir, and let sit for 15 minutes. Drain the vinegar (we think this gives just the right amount of acidity) and reserve (in case you want to add it back in). Add the remaining ingredients to the jar and stir well. Season with a nice pinch of salt and a couple grinds of pepper, stir again, and taste; it should have a nice balance of acidity, salinity, and herby freshness. If it tastes too harsh, add a few more splashes of olive oil. If you want it punchier, add a bit of the vinegar back in. It'll keep refrigerated for up to 5 days.

To make the sweet potatoes, bring a large pot of salted water to boil (it should taste like the sea). Cook the sweet potatoes, stirring to ensure they're cooking evenly, until they're soft enough to pierce with a knife, but not so soft that they break apart. Drain and set aside to cool, then halve lengthwise. Preheat a grill or heat a cast-iron pan over high heat. If using a cast-iron pan, pour in a few healthy glugs of olive oil. Place the potatoes cut side down and cook until caramel in color and lightly crisp. Be careful not to let the sweet potatoes burn.

To serve, gently pile the sweet potatoes on a platter, season with salt, and generously spoon the salsa verde over the top. Season to taste, sprinkle the lemon zest over the top, and serve.

KIMCHI FRIED RICE

This is perfect hangover food. It also hits the spot when you feel a cold coming on, as kimchi is, above all, bracing. This recipe is also a great way to use up leftover brisket from last night's dinner party.

2 teaspoons butter

1 cup braised beef brisket (see recipe), shredded

1 cup cooked rice (cooked in kimchi liquid; see note)

1 teaspoon sesame oil

pinch of salt

1 or 2 eggs, either stirred in, fried, or poached (optional)

1 or 2 spoonfuls chopped kimchi

1 teaspoon sesame seeds

———

Serves 1

In a wide skillet or wok, melt the butter over medium high heat until it starts to brown. When it's deep gold, add the brisket and cook to warm through for about 1 minute. Add the cooked rice and cook over high heat until it is piping hot. Stir in the sesame oil, season with salt.

As for the eggs, if using, you may stir one into the rice over high heat, or top the finished dish with either a fried egg or two poached eggs.

As for the kimchi, some people like a spoonful or two stirred into the rice; some prefer it on the side.

Just before serving, scatter the sesame seeds over the top.

WHAT YOU NEED TO KNOW

This fried rice recipe serves one but is easily doubled or tripled, depending on the size of your pan or wok. Add peas or baby spinach if you want to add a little green. I've included my recipe for brisket too. It's delicious for dinner with mashed potatoes and roasted carrots.

You'll need one jar of store-bought kimchi for this recipe. Drain the kimchi and reserve the liquid. You'll have about ¼ cup liquid. Replace ¼ cup of the water for cooking the rice with the ¼ cup of this potent liquid. Save the drained kimchi to use in this recipe, and serve extra on the side, as a condiment.

Braised Beef Brisket Serves 8

1 beef brisket, first cut (about 4 pounds)

olive oil, as needed

kosher salt and freshly cracked black pepper

5 carrots, peeled

4 red onions, halved

2 celery stalks, trimmed

3 garlic cloves, peeled

1 bay leaf

2 cups red wine

2 cups beef stock

Preheat the oven to 325°F.

Pat the brisket dry and rub it with a touch of olive oil. Season generously with salt and pepper.

In a Dutch oven, sear the brisket over medium-high heat until both sides are crusty brown. Add the carrots, onions, celery, garlic, and bay leaf. Pour in the wine and stock, turn the heat to high, and bring the liquid to a simmer. Cover with a heavy lid or aluminum foil, transfer to the oven, and bake for 3 to 4 hours, or until the brisket is easily cut with a fork.

Transfer the brisket to a cutting board. Slice the brisket across the grain at a diagonal or, for fried rice, shred it when it's cool enough to handle. Meanwhile, reduce the wine and stock over high heat until it is unctuous.

NIGHT FARE

FOUR SEASONS OF SPOONBREAD

This recipe blew me away. I've had good spoonbread before, but never this good. It's as light as a soufflé, as gentle as a pudding, and still strong enough to stand up to Dunsmoor's pronounced accompaniments. It makes for a lovely meal with a salad of tender greens. It also happens to be kind of perfect on its own with a cup of coffee and the newspaper on Sunday morning. A little research suggests that this American classic was named spoonbread because it is akin to a cornbread yet soft enough to eat with a spoon, but I think it's because the cook stood, spoon in hand, eating it straight from the pan.

3½ tablespoons butter, at room temperature

2 cups whole milk

⅓ cup fine cornmeal

1¼ teaspoons kosher salt

½ teaspoon pepper

3 eggs, separated

3 tablespoons grated Parmesan

———

Serves 4

Preheat the oven to 350°F. Butter an oven-safe 8-inch square baking dish with ½ tablespoon of the butter.

Heat the milk in a saucepan over low heat until warm. Remove from the heat. Whisk in the cornmeal, salt, and pepper and whisk continuously for 3 minutes. Add the remaining 3 tablespoons butter and continue to whisk until incorporated. Whisk in the egg yolks and set aside.

In a mixing bowl or stand mixer, beat the egg whites until they reach stiff peaks. With a rubber spatula, fold the whites into the cornmeal mixture until just combined. Fold in the Parmesan.

Gently pour the batter into the buttered dish. Bake for 20 to 25 minutes, or until the spoonbread has risen and the center has set. Serve immediately.

WHAT YOU NEED TO KNOW

Georgia-born Dunsmoor serves his spoonbread year-round, with a seasonal rotation of accompaniments. Some of the winter mushrooms he uses may be hard to find. If so, simply create your own mix of available wild mushrooms. You may add a tablespoon of minced chives or scallions directly to the batter before baking the spoonbread.

The only trick here is timing. Have the accompaniments ready and still hot just before the spoonbread is due to come out of the oven. Everything should be served immediately upon being cooked.

Blue Crab, Spring Peas, and Vermouth Spring Variation

3½ tablespoons sliced scallions or green garlic

1 cup dry vermouth

½ cup vegetable or chicken stock

½ cup cold butter, cut into pieces

¼ cup heavy cream

8 ounces lump crab meat

8 ounces blanched spring peas

freshly squeezed lemon juice, to taste

salt and pepper

Add 2 tablespoons of the scallions to the basic spoonbread recipe before baking.

Pour the vermouth into a large sauté pan and bring to a boil over high heat. Cook until the vermouth is reduced by two-thirds, then pour in the stock and bring to a boil again. Whisk in the cold butter, one piece at a time and then the cream. Whisk until emulsified. Add the crab meat, peas, and the remaining scallions. Lower the heat and gently simmer, stirring, for 1 minute. Add lemon juice, salt, and pepper to taste. Serve immediately to the side of the hot spoonbread.

Chanterelle Mushroom, Sweet Corn, and Chervil Summer Variation

1 pound corn kernels, cut off the cob

2 tablespoons chopped fresh chives

10 tablespoons cold butter, cut into pieces

8 ounces chanterelle mushrooms, trimmed and sliced

salt

½ cup dry vermouth

½ cup dry sherry

½ cup mushroom or chicken stock

¼ cup sour cream or crème fraîche

freshly squeezed lemon juice, to taste

pepper

½ cup fresh chervil leaves (optional)

Add half of the corn kernels and 1 tablespoon of the chives to the basic spoonbread recipe before baking.

In a large sauté pan, melt 2 tablespoons of the butter over medium heat. Add the mushrooms, season with salt, and sauté for 2 minutes. Add the vermouth and sherry, bring to a boil, and cook until reduced by two-thirds. Add the stock and the remaining corn kernels and bring to a boil again. Whisking, add the remaining 8 tablespoons butter, piece by piece, followed by the sour cream. Continue to cook until the sauce is emulsified and slightly thickened. Season with the lemon juice, salt, and pepper to taste. Sprinkle with the remaining chives. Just before serving, so that it doesn't wilt, garnish with the chervil. Serve immediately to the side of the hot spoonbread.

Sweet Potato, Porcini, and Madeira Autumn Variation

1 sweet potato, cut into ¼-inch dice

½ cup fresh huckleberries or dried currants

1 cup Madeira

10 tablespoons cold butter, cut into pieces

8 ounces fresh porcini mushrooms, cut into ¼-inch dice

1½ tablespoons fresh thyme

salt

½ cup white wine

½ cup mushroom or chicken stock

¼ cup sour cream or crème fraîche

freshly squeezed lemon juice, to taste

pepper

Blanch the sweet potato in boiling water for 3 minutes, then drain, pass under cold water, and pat dry. Add the sweet potato to the basic spoonbread recipe before baking.

Place the huckleberries in a small bowl. Warm ½ cup of the Madeira in a small saucepan over low heat, then pour over the berries. Let sit for 5 minutes to soften, stirring occasionally. Strain, reserving both the liquid and berries separately.

In a large sauté pan, melt 2 tablespoons of the butter over medium heat. Turn the heat to high and add the mushrooms and 1½ teaspoons of the thyme. Season with salt and sauté for 2 minutes, Add the wine and the remaining ½ cup Madeira, bring to a boil, and cook until reduced by two-thirds. Add the stock and bring to a boil again. Whisking, add the remaining 8 tablespoons butter, piece by piece, followed by the sour cream. Continue to cook until the sauce is emulsified and slightly thickened. Add the berries and cook just until warmed through. Season to taste with the lemon juice, salt, and pepper. Garnish with the remaining 1 tablespoon thyme. Serve immediately with the hot spoonbread.

Wild Mushrooms Winter Variation

1 tablespoon minced fresh chives

10 tablespoons cold butter, cut into pieces

12 ounces assorted fresh wild mushrooms (preferably a combination of hen of the woods, oyster, brown beech, and pioppini)

salt

½ cup white wine

½ cup dry vermouth

½ cup mushroom or chicken stock

¼ cup sour cream or crème fraîche

½ cup grated Parmesan, plus 1 cup shaved Parmesan

pepper

freshly squeezed lemon juice, to taste

1½ cups fresh herbs (preferably a combination of parsley, chives, dill, chervil, and tarragon)

olive oil

Add the minced chives to the basic spoonbread recipe before baking, if so desired.

In a large sauté pan, melt 2 tablespoons of the butter over medium heat. Turn the heat to high and add the mushrooms. Season with salt and sauté for 2 minutes. Add the wine and vermouth, bring to a boil, and cook until reduced by two-thirds. Add the stock and bring to a boil again. Whisking, add the remaining 8 tablespoons butter, piece by piece, followed by the sour cream and grated Parmesan. Continue to cook until the sauce is emulsified and slightly thickened. Season to taste with the salt, pepper, and lemon juice.

In a bowl, toss the herbs with a squeeze of lemon juice and olive oil.

Garnish with the shaved Parmesan and herb salad. Serve next to the hot spoonbread.

HATCHET HALL

If it were up to Brian Dunsmoor, he'd do away with all modern appliances. And, by that I mean, no stove. Anywhere. He is a man of the hearth, and in that hearth is a raging fire, the moods and temperature fluctuations of which he knows as if they were his own. Hatchet Hall is more than a throwback to another time, despite the taxidermy, wallpaper, and thrift-shop china. It is a committed, poetic ode to a colonial-era way of life, its forgotten spirits, indigenous varietals, and public meeting houses. That it should be in Los Angeles, the grande dame of artifice, is both inconceivable and utterly perfect.

ON SILVERTON AND GOIN

Most shifts in the culinary landscape of a city happen gradually. A few good restaurants open, and slowly the city's food scene starts to improve. Not so, for Los Angeles. The bold food we see in the city today appeared so suddenly that much of the country has yet to recognize this dramatic change. More surprising still is that this shift was not confined to one area, but rather bloomed with hothouse speed across the sprawling metropolis, from the canyons in the east to the beaches of the west. You might call it a zeitgeist moment. But, of course, as with all change, there's a story behind it and a bit of history.

A revolution, even a culinary one, needs its leaders, and much of the best food in Los Angeles today can be traced back to two seminal chefs: Nancy Silverton and Suzanne Goin. Most of the dozens of chefs I interviewed for this book, from Travis Lett of Gjelina to Josiah Citrin of Charcoal and Melisse to Emily Fiffer and Heather Sperling of Botanica and Jessica Koslow of Sqirl spoke of Nancy Silverton and Suzanne Goin with intimate, urgent reverence. They are the origin story for so many who have broken ground and broken bread in this city. Of course, Silverton is quick to credit her own mentor, Wolfgang Puck. And Goin, who worked for Silverton, is quick to credit Silverton. But the food we are seeing and eating in Los Angeles today doesn't hearken back to Puck's elaborate dishes. If anything, the model has been flipped.

Nancy Silverton has been a fixture in the Los Angeles food world since she and her then husband Mark Peel helped Wolfgang Puck open Spago in 1982. Puck had wisely made Silverton his pastry chef, but her first move was not to work on the dessert menu, but rather to rethink the bread being served at even the very best restaurants in Los Angeles. It was made from a powdered mix. You simply added water and called it a day. This was decidedly not Silverton's style of baking, and with truly obsessive dedication, she set her mind to creating a loaf that would rival those she had eaten in Europe. Spago became famous for many things, including Puck's smoked salmon pizzas, his Wiener schnitzel, Silverton's desserts—and her outstanding bread. And, in the 1980s, Spago was all the rage. A relentless parade of celebrities came to see and be seen and perhaps even to nibble sparingly at the rich food. By the time Silverton and Peel had had their first child, they were desperate for a month of quiet and peace, which they found in Italy.

Put two chefs in a house in the Italian countryside for a month, and chances are dinner will be good. But it was more than good. It was, for Silverton and Peel, an education in simplicity. And when it came time to return home to Los Angeles, they knew they wanted to continue to cook as they had been cooking all month in Italy.

For Silverton and Peel, cooking had become a means to let good ingredients shine. Not to mask purity with extravagant gestures and technique, but rather to present beautiful produce in its most natural form, with only a little help from olive oil, seasoning, herbs, and, where needed, a bit of heat. Like Alice Waters, they wanted to celebrate simplicity. Today, this approach doesn't sound so very radical. But when they returned to Los Angeles and opened Campanile, it seemed revolutionary. And when just next door, they opened La Brea Bakery and began selling Silverton's rustic bread, the city went mad for it. No one, save more recently Chad Robertson of Tartine Bakery in San Francisco, has had a greater impact on the baking of bread in this country.

Regulars devoured the fresh pasta, polenta, and risotto at Campanile, not to mention the lamb shanks, grilled steaks and flattened chicken. It was rustic, lusty, peasant fare made by true professionals. Moreover it was neither casual nor fancy exactly, but somewhere in between, and that zone, that midpoint, did

away with the stiff formalities of fine dining. People came to Campanile to eat well, drink well, and have fun.

It was around this time that a young native Angeleno, Suzanne Goin, returned home after working at a series of extraordinary restaurants, including Arpège in Paris and Chez Panisse in Berkeley. In 1995, she went to work at Campanile as a sous chef but was quickly promoted to chef de cuisine. Her prodigious talent and quiet, confident authority were immediately recognizable, and no one was surprised to see her soon looking for a space of her own. Her plans solidified when she was introduced to Caroline Styne, a young restaurateur and wine director. The two women became fast friends and partners. To this day, they finish each other's sentences with the ease of sisters. And, in 1998, they opened Lucques.

Lucques is a beautiful ode to the Mediterranean. And while the flavors of Italy, France, and Spain predominate, the influences of Morocco, Greece, and Turkey are never far off. Goin's cooking is rustic, bold, generous—enormously so, in fact. She is an assertive chef, whose food is brilliantly nuanced while never falling into a too-quiet refinement. I fell in love with her cooking, not in Los Angeles originally, but in Boston, at Olives Restaurant, and in Rhode Island, at Al Forno. I was a student at Harvard at the time, and those were the two restaurants that I would beg, borrow, and nearly steal to go to for any celebratory dinner or mere chance to escape the cafeteria. Al Forno meant a 45-minute drive from Cambridge and a long wait to get a table, but the restaurant served a deconstructed asparagus lasagna that was no more (and no less!) than a sheet of fresh pasta brushed in brown butter, showered with Parmesan and cracked black pepper, and gently folded around tender stalks of spring asparagus. It was a revelation. Years later, when I chanced upon the Chanterelle Lasagna with English Peas and Parmesan Pudding (page 122) at Lucques, Goin's evolution as a chef became apparent to me. It was a more complex dish, with warm blankets of flavor and textures meant to surprise and satisfy more robustly, but, at its core, there was still that reverence for ingredients and a willingness to let them take center stage.

Campanile is long closed and La Brea Bakery sold, but Silverton's more recent restaurants, Osteria Mozza, Pizzeria Mozza, and Chi Spacca, are a return to her month in Italy. Outstanding ingredients pared down to their essential essence. Meanwhile, Goin, now also the chef-owner of A.O.C. and the Larder, has started to bring the spices and sauces from her travels back to Los Angeles. And yet, however exotic her discoveries, in her hands, they fold seamlessly into her Mediterranean fare, working behind the scenes to lend yet another dimension, element of surprise, and rush of pleasure.

Suzanne Goin of Lucques, Melrose

CHANTERELLE LASAGNA WITH ENGLISH PEAS AND PARMESAN PUDDING

In this beauty of a spring dish, Goin has given a delicate lightness and deft refinement to what is usually the heartiest of pastas—baked lasagna. The miraculous result is rich without being heavy and as much an offering of farm-fresh spring peas, asparagus, and chanterelle mushrooms as it is about delectable sheets of pasta and seriously indulgent Parmesan cream. This, to me, whispers Easter Sunday, Mother's Day, the first sighting of daffodils, and the first whiff of hyacinth. It may be too time-consuming to make more than two or three times a year, but it is too good not to become an annual ritual.

PEA PUREE

½ cup olive oil

2 tablespoons butter

1 chile de arbol, crushed

1 sprig mint

1 garlic clove, minced

3 cups shelled English peas

generous pinch of sugar

¾ teaspoon salt

pepper

PARMESAN PUDDING

¾ cup melted butter

¾ cup all-purpose flour

3¾ cups whole milk

1¼ cups heavy cream

2 eggs plus 1 yolk

2¼ cups grated Parmesan

½ teaspoon kosher salt

pinch of pepper

PARMESAN CREAM

2 cups heavy cream

1 cup grated Parmesan

¼ teaspoon salt

¼ teaspoon pepper

LASAGNA

1 cup fresh bread crumbs

5 tablespoons olive oil

1½ pounds chanterelle or morel mushrooms

2 tablespoons diced shallots

sea salt

pepper

1 tablespoon fresh thyme leaves

2 cups English peas

2 cups sugar snap peas, sliced on a diagonal

2 cups thin asparagus, sliced on a diagonal

2 cups cherry tomatoes, halved

1 cup English pea tendrils (optional), plus more for garnish

1 (1-pound) box lasagna noodles

1 tablespoon butter

chives, for garnish (optional)

To make the pea puree, heat a medium saucepan over low heat. Add the olive oil, butter, chile de arbol, and mint. Let sizzle for a minute, then stir in the garlic. Let the garlic sizzle for another minute, then stir in the peas, sugar, and salt. Season with pepper and simmer for about 5 minutes, stirring occasionally, until the peas are just tender. Strain, reserving the oil-butter mixture. Discard the chile and mint.

Transfer the peas to a food processor and process until nearly smooth. With the motor running, pour in the reserved oil-butter mixture slowly and process until creamy but still textured. Season with salt and pepper to taste. Keep warm.

To make the Parmesan pudding, preheat the oven to 325°F. Bring a kettle of water to a boil.

Set a saucepan over medium heat and make a roux by whisking together the melted butter and flour. Add the milk and cream, whisk to combine, and cook until the mixture is warm to the touch. Remove from the heat and add the eggs and yolk, whisking constantly until the eggs are integrated. Stir in the Parmesan, salt, and pepper.

Pour the custard into a baking dish and cover with a tight layer of plastic wrap followed by a layer of aluminum foil. Place the covered baking dish in a larger baking dish. Pour the boiling water into the larger baking dish to create a bain-marie. The water should come about two-thirds of the way up the baking dish with the custard. Bake for 1½ hours, or until just set.

To make the Parmesan cream, bring the cream to a simmer over low heat and whisk in the Parmesan until incorporated. Remove from the heat and stir in the salt and pepper. Taste and adjust the seasoning if necessary. Set aside somewhere warm.

To make the lasagna, turn the oven to 375°F. Bring a large pot of salted water to a boil.

continued

Serves 6

Lasagna, continued

Place the bread crumbs in a bowl and toss with 1 table-spoon of the olive oil until well coated. Transfer bread crumbs to a rimmed baking sheet and toast, stirring often, for 10 to 12 minutes, or until they are golden brown. Set aside.

Warm 2 tablespoons of the olive oil in a large skillet over high heat. Wait for it to smoke a bit, then add the mushrooms. Cook, stirring, until the mushrooms are tender and slightly crispy. Add the shallots, 1 teaspoon salt, and a pinch of pepper and cook for 1 minute more. Stir in the thyme.

Add the remaining 2 tablespoons olive oil to the mushrooms, followed by the English peas, sugar snaps, asparagus, and cherry tomatoes and cook over low heat until the peas and asparagus are just tender to the bite, about 5 minutes. Season with ½ teaspoon of salt and a pinch of pepper. Remove from the heat and, at the last moment, add the pea tendrils (if using). Gently toss the pea tendrils until coated in the olive oil, being careful not to let them wilt.

Cook the pasta in the boiling water until just tender, or according to the directions on the package. Drain and toss with the butter.

To assemble the lasagna, start with the pea puree, add a layer of pasta, then Parmesan pudding, then vegetables. Repeat once. Top the last sheet of pasta with vegetables. Spoon the hot Parmesan cream over the top and scatter with the toasted bread crumbs and chives.

WHAT YOU NEED TO KNOW

If you can't locate a source of pea tendrils, simply add a bit more of the peas and asparagus. Goin's brilliant move here is not to bake the lasagna, but to simply assemble the cooked components so that they maintain their freshness. At the restaurant, she plates individual portions, but, at home, it makes far more sense to make one large lasagna on a platter and garnish it with additional tendrils, toasted bread crumbs, and perhaps some chopped chives. I've tried to list steps in a clear, productive order, but read the whole recipe first and do things like set the pasta pot of water to a boil while working on the other components. The pea puree may be made in advance and reheated in a microwave or double boiler.

Emily Fiffer and Heather Sperling of Botanica, Silver Lake

CASSOULET VERT

This dish answers the question: can the transporting effect of cassoulet be achieved without the essential magic of pork sausage and duck confit? The answer is a resounding yes! The secret is in building layer upon layer of vibrant flavors. A garden's worth of aromatics are cooked down to create an intensely flavorful base to which heirloom beans are added. The final dish is served with a triple dose of herbaceousness: an herbal pistou, a garlicky gremolata, and a vibrant, herb-filled salad. But the true beauty of this recipe for me lies in the use of Pernod, fennel, and fennel seeds, giving the cassoulet a faint haunting of licorice.

BEANS

4 cups dried cannellini beans

8 cups vegetable stock

sachet of 3 star anise, ¼ cup black peppercorns, 2 tablespoons toasted fennel seeds, and 3 chiles de arbol

small handful of kosher salt

CASSOULET

1½ cups coarsely chopped yellow onion

1½ cups coarsely chopped shallots

olive oil

salt

2 cups coarsely chopped leek, white and light green parts only

1 cup sliced scallion, white and light green parts only

1 cup diced green chile

⅓ cup coarsely chopped garlic

¼ teaspoon toasted fennel seeds, finely ground

1 teaspoon ground cloves

¼ cup Pernod, plus a splash more

2 cups coarsely chopped celery

2 cups coarsely chopped fennel

2 cups coarsely chopped parsnip

1 tablespoon chopped fresh thyme

½ cup fino sherry

⅓ cup sherry vinegar

½ (750 ml) bottle dry white wine, plus more as needed

½ lemon

PISTOU

½ cup fresh basil

½ cup fresh flat-leaf parsley

½ cup fresh dill

½ cup fennel fronds

2 garlic cloves

2 cups olive oil

¼ cup freshly squeezed lemon juice

a good sprinkle of salt

GREMOLATA

olive oil

2 tablespoons minced garlic

¼ cup finely chopped fresh parsley

2 tablespoons grated lemon zest

TO SERVE

ground toasted fennel seed and pink peppercorns

spring vegetables, greens, and herbs (shaved asparagus, celery leaves, parsley, pea tendrils, slivered snap peas, frilly mustard greens)

lemon juice

olive oil

salt

Serves 6

To make the beans, soak the beans in the stock overnight.

Place the beans and their soaking stock in a large pot and set over high heat. Add the sachet, bring to a simmer, and cook gently for a few hours, until the beans are just cooked through. Once the beans lose their initial hardness, season with the salt. The beans are done when they still hold their shape but are tender enough to eat with pleasure. Set aside to cool in their cooking liquid; do not drain.

To make the cassoulet, in a food processor, whizz the onion and shallots into a fine paste. Pour plenty of olive oil into a large sauté pan and set over high heat. Add the onion-shallot mixture and ¼ teaspoon of salt. Cook, stirring constantly, until the alliums start to caramelize and turn golden.

Combine the leek, scallion, green chile, and garlic in the food processor and whizz into a fine paste. Add the leek mixture to the pan and add another ¼ teaspoon of salt. Cook, stirring constantly, until, again, the mixture starts to caramelize.

Add the ground fennel seeds and cloves. Add the Pernod and deglaze the skillet. Turn the heat to medium and cook for a few minutes or until the alcohol has mostly evaporated.

continued

Pulse the celery, fennel, and parsnip in the food processor until the vegetables are finely chopped.

Add a little more olive oil to the skillet, followed by the finely chopped vegetables and the thyme. Add another ¼ teaspoon salt and stir to combine. Turn the heat to medium-low and cook until soft, caramelized, and slightly jam-like, about 40 minutes.

Turn the heat to high and add the fino sherry and sherry vinegar and stir to incorporate. Turn the heat to medium again and cook for about 10 more minutes.

Turn the heat back to high and add the white wine. Reduce the heat to low and simmer for about 30 minutes. The mixture should still be solidly wet. If it looks dry, add more wine.

Add the cooked beans with a slotted spoon and enough of the bean cooking liquid to cover. Gently cook the cassoulet over low heat until the ingredients come together, the beans are completely cooked through, and the whole thing has a beautiful stew-like consistency. Add a good splash of Pernod and a squeeze of fresh lemon juice.

To make the pistou, combine all of the ingredients in a blender and blend until nearly smooth. Set aside.

To make the gremolata, pour a little bit of olive oil into a small pan and set over high heat. Add the garlic and cook, stirring, until golden brown. Pour off the olive oil. Transfer the garlic to a small bowl along with the parsley and lemon zest and stir.

To serve, put the hot cassoulet into a clay cassole or cazuela or warmed shallow serving bowl. Garnish with gremolata, a generous dollop of pistou, and a dusting of ground toasted fennel seed and pink peppercorns. Top with a small salad of spring vegetables, greens, and herbs dressed in lemon juice, olive oil, and salt.

WHAT YOU NEED TO KNOW

Cooking the cannellinis from scratch is a must. It infuses the beans with flavor and yields a rich cooking liquid, which is then stirred into the cassoulet. A spunky, natural red wine to drink with the dish is also a must, as is a hunk of crusty bread, toasted, rubbed with a cut garlic clove, brushed with good olive oil, and showered with sea salt.

SPICY FUSILLI

The key to Shook and Dotolo's success is that they make the food you want to eat and they make it really well. It's that simple. And what could be simpler than a bowl of pasta with a vodka tomato sauce? Add a crazy amount of butter and cream, and you have the richest version you've ever tasted—and undoubtedly the best. Thankfully, it's still fabulous with half that butter and cream. I'm giving you the real deal restaurant version here, with a note on where to cut back if you want to indulge blissfully, but not obscenely.

VODKA TOMATO SAUCE

⅔ cup olive oil

2 garlic cloves, finely chopped

2 shallots, finely chopped

5 (4½-ounce) tubes tomato paste

¼ cup vodka

2½ cups heavy cream

1 tablespoon red pepper flakes

salt

SPICY FUSILLI

1 pound fusilli or another short pasta shape

2 sticks (1 cup) butter

1 cup heavy cream

2¼ cups Vodka Tomato Sauce (see recipe)

salt and pepper

pinch of red pepper flakes

16 basil leaves, torn up a bit

grated Parmesan, to pass at the table

Serves 4, sauce makes 4½ cups

To make the tomato sauce, heat the olive oil in a wide skillet over medium heat. Add the garlic and shallots and sweat. Add the tomato paste, stir to combine, and cook for a few minutes; it will turn a rusty color. Add the vodka and carefully ignite it with a match to flambé it. Do not blow the flame out; it will die off once the alcohol has evaporated. Add the cream and cook, whisking to combine, for 3 minutes. Stir in the pepper flakes and season with salt. Keep about 2¼ cups in the skillet and reserve the rest for another use.

To make the fusilli, bring a large pot of salted water to a boil. Cook the pasta until al dente and drain, reserving some of the cooking water.

Meanwhile, over medium heat, add half the butter and cream to the tomato sauce. Taste and add more cream and butter until it tastes as rich as you want it. Stir to combine. Season with salt, pepper, and chili flakes.

Add the cooked pasta to the sauce and toss over medium heat. Slowly stream in a few spoonfuls of the cooking water to emulsify the sauce, if needed. Stir in the basil. Check the seasonings. Serve in warmed shallow bowls and pass the Parmesan at the table.

WHAT YOU NEED TO KNOW

There's enough sauce here to freeze half and use half. And you will want this dish again soon. Part of what makes this sauce so very good is the use of tomato paste instead of plum tomatoes. It gives a concentrated taste. It's also a shortcut, as you won't need to cook the tomatoes down.

PAN-SEARED HALIBUT WITH FRESH CORN GRITS AND CALABRIAN CHILE SAUCE

When I asked chef Williams why he decided to call his restaurant Norah, his answer was true to his deep-rooted sense of humility. "I wanted an American name that wasn't pretentious, and I liked the sound of it." Williams is never one to lead with a list of his accomplishments, but anyone who eats his food is bound to realize that the list is long. It also includes active duty in Iraq shortly after 9/11 as a marine. Traveling the world has led Williams to pair the unexpected, and here, a simple pan-seared halibut is given heat with chiles from Calabria, Italy, and served with fresh corn grits that reflect his love of Southern cooking.

CALABRIAN CHILE SAUCE

1 (12-ounce) jar oil-packed Calabrian chiles

2 tablespoons red wine vinegar

1½ tablespoons water

1½ teaspoons sugar

1 teaspoon salt

FRESH CORN GRITS

6 to 8 ears of yellow corn, shucked

water, as needed

2 tablespoons butter

1 teaspoon salt

HALIBUT

4 (6-ounce) skinless halibut fillets

kosher salt

3 tablespoons grapeseed oil

3 tablespoons butter, cut into pieces

2 lemons, to squeeze

Serves 4

WHAT YOU NEED TO KNOW

If your halibut is very thick, finish cooking it in a 350°F oven. Save any remaining chile oil for another use—pizza, pasta, eggs and avocado toast are good matches.

To make the chile sauce, drain the chiles, reserving the oil. If whole, remove their seeds and stems. Combine the seeded chiles with the remaining ingredients in a blender and blend until smooth. With the blender running, slowly pour in about half of the reserved chile oil in a thin steady stream, to emulsify the sauce.

To make the fresh corn grits, use the large holes of a box grater and grate the kernels off the shucked ears of corn. You will need 2 full cups of grated kernels. Save any accumulated milky liquid for the dish.

Transfer the kernels and their milk to a skillet that's wide enough to fit the corn in a single layer. Cook over medium-low heat, stirring constantly, until the corn turns a dark gold and is smooth, 10 to 15 minutes. You may need to add a splash of water now and then if it gets too thick; lower the heat if it begins to scorch. Once the consistency is of creamy grits or risotto and the color has deepened, add the butter and sea salt and stir well to combine. Remove from the heat and set aside. Cover to keep warm.

To make the halibut, pat the fillets dry with paper towels and season with kosher salt.

Warm a stainless steel or nonstick sauté pan over medium-high heat. The pan should be wide enough to fit all of the fish fillets spaced 1 inch apart, or you can cook the fish in two batches. Pour the grapeseed oil into the hot pan; it should shimmer and smoke lightly. If the oil doesn't smoke a little, turn the heat to high and wait for it to get hotter. If the oil is smoking too much, remove the pan from the heat, discard the burned oil, wipe the pan clean, and start over.

When the oil is hot, sear the fish until a golden crust forms, about 2 to 3 minutes. Turn the heat to medium and flip the fish to cook the other side. Add the butter to the pan. It will immediately melt, bubble, and foam up; use the melted butter to continuously baste the fish. Cook for 2 minutes, or until just cooked through. Remove the pan from the heat, give the fish a squeeze of lemon juice and a drizzle of the Calabrian chile sauce, and serve immediately, from the pan, with the corn grits.

SALMON IN BACON MISO BROTH

This is umami! It's as simple as making a bacon miso broth and serving it in wide bowls over salmon. The broth is absurdly good—you may be temped to skip the salmon and drink it straight from a ladle.

½ cup applewood smoked bacon, cut into lardons

½ cup garlic cloves, peeled

1 jalapeño chile, halved lengthwise and seeded

3 scallions

½ yellow onion

½ cup peeled and sliced fresh ginger

2 stalks lemongrass

4 cups chicken stock (preferably homemade)

¼ cup white miso

½ sheet kombu

handful of bonito flakes

4 (6-ounce) salmon fillets, skin removed

3 scallions, cut into ribbons

———

Serves 4

Put the bacon in a stockpot and cook over medium heat. When the bacon begins to render its fat, add the garlic. Continue to cook, stirring from time to time, for a few more minutes until nearly crisp.

Meanwhile, either under a broiler or on a grill, char the jalapeño, scallions, and onion until they start to blacken on all sides.

Add the charred jalapeño, scallions, and onion to the stockpot, followed by the ginger, lemongrass, stock, and miso and whisk to combine. Bring to a boil, then lower the heat and simmer for 30 minutes. Remove from the heat. Add the kombu and bonito flakes and let steep for 10 minutes. Strain into a pot and keep hot over low heat.

Fill a roasting or poaching pan with water and bring to a boil. Lower the heat to a simmer, add the salmon fillets, and cover the pan. Poach the fish for 5 minutes, or until just opaque. Remove and discard the poaching liquid.

Place each salmon fillet in a wide bowl. Ladle a generous amount of hot broth on top. Garnish with a few ribbons of scallions and serve immediately.

GOLDEN TROUT WITH HAZELNUTS AND BROWN BUTTER

This is a riff on a French classic, *truite amandine*, in which trout is served with toasted almond slices and browned butter. Here, Fraser adds ginger, raisins, and capers to create a sweet and sour sauce. It's particularly good with wilted spinach and quinoa or couscous.

¾ cup butter, plus more as needed

⅓ cup chopped toasted hazelnuts

⅓ cup finely chopped shallots

¼ cup finely chopped fresh ginger

¼ cup chopped fresh parsley

¼ cup golden raisins, plumped in warm water for 1 minute, then drained

3 tablespoons capers, drained and rinsed

zest and juice of 1½ lemons

salt and pepper

canola oil, as needed

4 (6-ounce) California golden trout fillets

2 lemons, halved

wilted spinach (see recipe)

Serves 4

In a medium saucepan, melt the butter over medium heat and continue to cook until it is a medium shade of brown. Add the hazelnuts, shallots, and ginger and stir to perfume the butter. Remove from the heat and stir in the parsley, raisins, capers, and lemon zest and juice. Season with salt and pepper to taste. Set aside; you will need to give this a stir and warm it right before serving.

In a large cast-iron or other heavy pan, pour in enough canola oil to lightly coat the bottom of the pan and set over medium heat. Carefully add 2 trout fillets, skin side down. Cook until the flesh turns opaque about halfway up the fish. Add a pat of butter and let it brown. Remove from the heat and baste the fish in the butter until just cooked through. Squeeze lemon juice over the fish and remove from the pan. Repeat with the remaining fish.

Serve with several spoonfuls of the brown butter sauce drizzled over the top and wilted spinach on the side.

WHAT YOU NEED TO KNOW

California golden trout is the state fish. Outside of California, it may be easier to source rainbow trout, which makes a good substitute. If you have two large pans, use them. Otherwise, you will need to cook the trout in two quick batches.

Wilted Spinach

4 shallots, minced

¼ cup olive oil

2 pounds spinach leaves

salt

zest of 2 lemons

In a large pot, sauté the shallots in the olive oil until tender. Add the spinach and cook until just wilted. Season with salt and stir in the lemon zest.

TURMERIC GRILLED SEA BASS

There's a purity to Vietnamese food and, in its refined elegance, a welcome simplicity. Here, the earthiness of turmeric and garlic and the heat of Thai chiles in the marinade are offset by an abundant bouquet of fresh herbs and a squeeze of lime. It couldn't be easier and it couldn't be better.

½ cup canola oil

2 teaspoons fish sauce

6 to 8 garlic cloves, peeled

1 to 3 Thai chiles

1½ teaspoons ground turmeric

2 sea bass (about 1¼ to 1½ pounds each), boned and butterflied

handful of fresh cilantro or micro cilantro leaves

handful of fresh mint leaves, slivered if large

handful of fresh dill leaves

handful of fresh laksa leaves (optional)

olive oil, for drizzling

1 lime, cut into wedges

—————

Serves 4

Combine the canola oil, fish sauce, garlic, Thai chiles, and turmeric in a Vitamix or food processor and process until pureed. Brush the marinade onto the fish, inside and out. Set aside for half an hour.

Grill the fish over medium-high heat, skin side first. After 4 minutes, or once the skin is brown and blistered, flip it. Continue to cook, skin side up, until the fish is barely cooked through, about 4 more minutes.

Transfer to a platter. Garnish lavishly with the herbs and drizzle with the olive oil. Serve immediately with the lime wedges.

WHAT YOU NEED TO KNOW

Red snapper or sea bream may be swapped in for the sea bass. Have your fishmonger remove the bones and vertebrae and butterfly the fish, leaving the head and tail attached. Laska leaf is also known as Vietnamese cilantro and Vietnamese mint, and, yes, it has notes of both. If it's hard to find, just add a few more sprigs of cilantro and mint. Thai chiles, also called bird's eye chiles, are hot, so add, taste, add, taste until you find your happy point. To make them a little milder, remove the seeds. The fish can be grilled, broiled, or seared on a grill pan.

Doug Miriello of Gesso, West Hollywood

CRISPY BRANZINO WITH BIRD'S EYE CHILE VINAIGRETTE

Miriello's pantry knows no borders. He's known for bringing his Jewish and Italian background to the farmers' markets of Los Angeles. It is indeed as hard to resist his grilled persimmon and burrata as it is his latke hash browns or, for that matter, his octopus puttanesca, but this crispy Thai fish is a favorite of mine. It's all in the vinaigrette, which will go immediately into that buzzing space in your head that holds cravings and triggers insatiable urges to mix French breakfast radishes with bird's eye chiles. Serve it with rice, preferably cooked in coconut milk.

BIRD'S EYE CHILE VINAIGRETTE

1 bunch French Breakfast radishes

3 to 5 birds's eye chiles, to taste

6 Fresno chiles

1 large shallot

6 garlic cloves, peeled

1 bunch cilantro, leaves picked

1 teaspoon kosher salt

zest and juice of 2 limes

¼ cup fish sauce

¼ cup rice vinegar

1 tablespoon honey

¼ cup grapeseed oil

FISH

1 cup rice flour

kosher salt and pepper

4 branzino, cleaned

peanut or canola oil, for frying

TO SERVE

4 limes, halved

1 bunch cilantro, leaves picked

1 bunch parsley, leaves picked

1 red onion, cut into paper-thin slices

2 Persian cucumbers, thinly sliced

Serves 4

WHAT YOU NEED TO KNOW

Have your fishmonger scale, gut, and clean your fish and, if you prefer, slice the fish into two fillets. If you do not have a mortar and pestle or molcajete, use the pulse button on a food processor when making the vinaigrette.

To make the vinaigrette, trim and finely dice the radishes, chiles, shallot, and garlic. Chop the cilantro leaves.

Using a mortar and pestle or molcajete, smash the garlic and salt into a paste. Add the chiles and pound for about a minute. Add the shallot and smash even more. (Don't add the shallot earlier or smash too aggressively, as it will become bitter.) Add the lime zest and cilantro, followed by the lime juice, radishes, fish sauce, rice vinegar, and honey. Work the ingredients together until well combined, then drizzle in the grapeseed oil.

To cook the fish, stir together the rice flour, 1 tablespoon salt, and ½ teaspoon pepper in a small bowl. Spread the seasoned flour into a thin layer on a tray or a large sheet of parchment paper. Pat the fish dry with paper towels, then dredge in the flour until both sides of the fish have a light coating. Give a little shake to remove any excess. Set aside while you dredge the remaining fish. Do not dredge in advance; dredge just before frying.

If you have a fryer, heat the oil to 350°F. Otherwise, pour a few inches of oil into a Dutch oven and set over high heat until the oil is hot.

Taking care not to burn yourself, lower one fish into the hot oil. Fry for approximately 5 minutes, or until done to your liking. Repeat with the remaining fish.

Carefully transfer the fried fish to a paper towel–lined tray to soak up any excess oil. Immediately sprinkle with a pinch of kosher salt. Squeeze the juice from ½ lime over each fish and drizzle with bird's eye chile vinaigrette.

Serve immediately with the remaining limes and garnish with cilantro, parsley, red onion, and cucumbers. Pour the remaining bird's eye chile vinaigrette into a bowl and pass at the table.

ROAST CHICKEN, CRISPY POTATOES, SHISHITOS, AJI VERDE AND LOVE SAUCE

Many a fine French restaurant will test a young chef seeking employment by having the nervous applicant make three basic dishes: an omelet, a salad, and a roast chicken. The trick to the omelet is to keep it yellow, with nary a brown spot. The trick to the salad lies in the ratio of dressing to greens, as the leaves must wear only a bare wisp of vinaigrette. And, finally, the trick to the roast chicken is moist, seasoned meat under crispy, browned skin.

Here, Hollingsworth doubles down on the chicken. Cooked at high heat, the skin crisps, as shishito peppers and cherry tomatoes are roasted alongside. But the real secret lies in what he calls his Love Sauce. And, yes, you will love it and brush it liberally on everything, including grilled bread. Here it adds flavor to the chicken skin while keeping the meat moist and flavorful.

LOVE SAUCE

3 heads garlic

5 tablespoons olive oil

2 cups white wine

1 teaspoon Aleppo pepper

ROAST CHICKEN

1 whole chicken (about 4 pounds)

salt and pepper

1 lemon, halved and seeded

1 head garlic, the outer, papery skin removed

1 cup shishito peppers

1 cup cherry tomatoes

1 bunch cilantro, leaves picked

crispy potatoes (see recipe), for serving

aji verde (see recipe), for serving

Serves 4

To make the love sauce, preheat the oven to 350°F.

Cut just enough from the top of each head of garlic to reveal the cloves. In a small oven-safe sauté pan, heat the olive oil over medium-low heat. Add the garlic, cut side down, and cook for 1 to 2 minutes, until the garlic is nicely browned. Pour in the wine, bring to a boil, and transfer the pan to the oven for about 30 minutes, or until the wine is reduced to about 3 tablespoons. Remove from the oven and set aside to cool.

When cool enough to handle, squeeze out the softened garlic cloves directly into the pan. Add the Aleppo pepper and use a whisk to crush the garlic and integrate it into the liquid. Store in an airtight container in the refrigerator for up to 1 week. Bring to room temperature and stir before using.

Turn the oven to 425°F.

To make the chicken, liberally season the inside of the chicken with salt and pepper, then stuff with the lemon halves and the head of garlic. Pat dry the chicken skin with paper towels. Season the skin with salt, then brush liberally with Love Sauce.

Roast the chicken in a spacious roasting pan for 45 minutes, then give it another liberal brushing of Love Sauce. Add the shishito peppers and cherry tomatoes to the roasting pan and toss them in the accumulated juices. Roast the chicken and vegetables for another 45 minutes, or until the thigh juices run clear. Remove from the oven.

Serve, surrounded by the crispy potatoes, shishitos, and cherry tomatoes. Drizzle with the pan juices and top with the cilantro. Pass a bowl of aji verde at the table.

continued

Crispy Potatoes

2 pounds potatoes (such as tricolor marble), scrubbed

peanut oil, for frying

zest of ½ lemon

1 tablespoon fleur de sel

1 tablespoon minced red onion

kosher salt and pepper

chopped fresh parsley, for serving

Preheat the oven to 350°F.

Place the whole potatoes on a rimmed baking sheet lined with parchment paper. Bake until the potatoes offer little resistance when pierced with a sharp, thin-bladed knife, 30 to 45 minutes, depending on their size. Set aside at room temperature until cool enough to handle. When cool, use the palm of your hand to slightly flatten the potatoes and break their skin a bit.

Pour 3 to 4 inches of oil into a heavy Dutch oven or other deep pot and set over medium-high heat until the oil reaches 400°F.

While the oil heats, in a small bowl, stir together the lemon zest and fleur de sel. Set aside.

Fry the potatoes, in batches if necessary, until evenly brown all over, about 3 minutes. Remove them with a spider skimmer or slotted spoon and transfer them directly to a large bowl. Adjust the heat as necessary between batches to return the oil to 400°F.

While the potatoes are still hot, gently toss with the red onion. Season with the lemon salt, kosher salt, and pepper to taste and toss again. Garnish with parsley and serve immediately.

Aji Verde

2 bunches cilantro, leaves picked

2 bunches scallions, trimmed

3 jalapeño chiles

2 serrano chiles

3 garlic cloves, peeled

½ cup freshly squeezed lime juice

½ cup mayonnaise

salt and pepper

Combine all of the ingredients in a blender and blend until smooth. (This may be made a few hours in advance, but its color will not be as vibrant when serving. Any longer than a few hours and the garlic will be too pungent.)

HARISSA CHICKEN WITH STEWED CHICKPEAS AND TZATZIKI

This is spicy comfort food, perfect for a cold night. Chef Miriello gives us a triple dose of harissa, first using it to marinate the chicken, then basting the chicken with it as it cooks, and then passing a bowl of it at the table. Not to worry, the tzatziki and stewed chickpeas counter the heat, and a generous shower of herbs and lemon juice keep it fresh.

2 cups whole Greek yogurt (such as Fage)

1 cup harissa (page 172)

juice of ¼ lemon

1 tablespoon salt

3 small whole roasting chickens (about 3 pounds each), butterflied and halved (see note)

grapeseed oil, as needed

½ cup roasted red bell peppers (optional)

1 bunch cilantro, leaves picked

1 bunch flat-leaf parsley, leaves picked

3 lemons, halved

stewed chickpeas (see recipe)

tzatziki (see recipe)

Serves 6 hungry people

Stir together the yogurt, ½ cup of the harissa, the lemon juice, and salt in a bowl. Coat the chicken in the yogurt mixture and let marinate in the fridge, covered, for 6 to 8 hours.

Preheat the oven to 400°F.

In a large cast-iron pan, pour in enough grapeseed oil to generously coat the bottom of the pan and set over high heat. Cook the chicken, skin side down, for about 3 minutes. Flip and cook the other side, basting the chicken with harissa. Flip and baste the chicken three more times; this should take about 15 minutes total. Transfer the chicken to the oven and roast for 25 to 30 minutes, or until juicy, tender, saucy, and charred.

Shower the chicken with the cilantro and parsley. Serve with the lemons, chickpeas, tzatziki, red bell peppers, if using, and additional harissa.

WHAT YOU NEED TO KNOW

To make this chicken, you will need to make the harissa on page 172 or use a harissa of your choosing. Couscous makes a good alternative to the stewed chickpeas if time is short. Sear the chicken in batches so as not to crowd the pan. To butterfly or spatchcock a chicken, have your butcher remove the backbone and flatten the chicken; this ensures even cooking. For this recipe, you will then cut each butterflied chicken into two halves.

continued

Stewed Chickpeas

3 cups dried chickpeas

olive oil, as needed

1 large yellow onion

1 large carrot

½ celery stalk

1 large shallot

1 Fresno chile

1 tomato

3 bay leaves

¼ cup garlic cloves

salt and pepper

freshly squeezed lemon juice, to taste

Soak the chickpeas in plenty of water overnight. The following day, drain the chickpeas. Roughly chop the vegetables.

In a heavy pot, heat a plentiful amount of oil. When it's hot, char the vegetables until they start to brown.

Add the aromatics and toast lightly. Add the soaked chickpeas, enough water to cover by a few inches, and 3 tablespoons of salt.

Bring to a bare boil and reduce the heat. Simmer for 1½ to 2 hours, or until the chickpeas are tender. Drain, reserving the cooking liquid.

With a large spoon, smash 2 cups of the cooked chickpeas with some of their hot cooking liquid and return them to the pot. Smash them enough to break them apart but not turn them to mash. Season with salt, pepper, and lemon juice. Drizzle with olive oil.

Tzatziki

4 Persian cucumbers

2 cups whole Greek yogurt (such as Fage)

2 garlic cloves, grated on a Microplane

¼ cup chopped fresh mint

¼ cup chopped fresh dill

2 teaspoons white wine vinegar

juice of 1 or 2 lemons

2 tablespoons kosher or table salt

½ teaspoon sea salt

½ teaspoon pepper

tiny pinch of cayenne pepper

Grate the cucumbers and toss them with the 2 tablespoons salt. Let them sit for 10 to 15 minutes in a colander. Rinse to remove the salt and drain. Pat dry. Combine with the remaining ingredients and refrigerate until ready to use.

BLISTERED GREEN BEANS AND SICHUAN PORK BELLY

A favorite weeknight supper. Serve with rice and cold beer.

8 ounces skinless pork belly

3 tablespoons salt

1 tablespoon sugar

1 tablespoon grapeseed oil

12 ounces green beans, trimmed

juice from 1 lime

8 fresh Thai basil leaves

SOY-CHILE SAUCE

½ cup low-sodium soy sauce

⅓ cup rice vinegar

2 tablespoons honey

1 Thai chile, minced

1 (5-inch) piece fresh ginger, peeled and minced

2 garlic cloves, minced

2 tablespoons water

2 tablespoons cornstarch

TO SERVE

2 radishes, thinly sliced

2 tablespoons toasted peanuts, crushed

2 teaspoons white or black sesame seeds

Serves 2 or 3

Rub the pork belly on all sides with the salt and sugar. Refrigerate, wrapped in plastic wrap, for at least 12 and up to 24 hours.

Preheat the oven to 350°F. Wash off the dry marinade and pat the pork dry with paper towels. Place the pork in a roasting pan. Roast for 2½ hours. Remove from the oven and let cool. When cool enough to handle, cut it into ½-inch cubes. The pork may be prepared to this point and refrigerated for up to 24 hours. Bring to room temperature before proceeding.

While the pork roasts, prepare the soy-chile sauce. In a small pot, combine the soy sauce, rice vinegar, honey, Thai chile, ginger and garlic. Bring to a simmer over low heat and cook for 5 minutes. Meanwhile, stir together the water and cornstarch in a small bowl to create a slurry. Whisk the slurry into the sauce, turn the heat to high, and bring to a boil. Cook, continuing to whisk, until the sauce thickens slightly. Remove from the heat and set aside until needed.

Heat the grapeseed oil in a wok over high heat until it begins to smoke. Add the green beans and cook until the skin begins to blister and the beans begin to wilt. Add the roasted pork belly and cook until heated through. Remove from the heat, then add the lime juice, Thai basil, and soy-chile sauce and toss together. Garnish with radishes, crushed peanuts, and sesame seeds. Serve.

WHAT YOU NEED TO KNOW

The pork needs to cure in a dry rub overnight, so plan ahead. But once the pork has been cured and cooked, you can have this on the table in less time than it takes to cook the rice. If you happen to have access to Sichuan peppercorns, add a few to the soy-chile sauce. They lend an almost floral note that will hover mysteriously in the background.

BALSAMIC BARBECUED BABY BACKS

Serve these ribs and watch even your most fastidious friends turn primal. Like so many of Shook and Dotolo's recipes, this one checks all the boxes: sweet, sour, spicy, boozy, finger-licking deliciousness. Theirs is a hold-nothing-back style of cooking that never fails to please.

BARBECUE SAUCE

1 (12-ounce) bottle lager-style beer

1 cup ketchup

½ cup balsamic vinegar

¼ cup water

1 red onion, diced

1 garlic clove, very finely chopped

½ packed cup light brown sugar

3 tablespoons honey

1½ tablespoons grainy mustard

1 to 2 teaspoons Tabasco

1 teaspoon Worcestershire sauce

RIBS

2 racks pork baby back ribs (about 4 pounds)

canola or grapeseed oil, as needed

salt

4 sprigs flat-leaf parsley

4 sprigs thyme

4 garlic cloves, peeled and smashed

Serves 4

To make the barbecue sauce, whisk all of the ingredients together in a medium saucepan and bring to a boil over medium-high heat. Turn the heat to medium-low, keeping the sauce at a bare simmer, and cook, partially covered, until as thick as ketchup, 2 to 3 hours.

To make the ribs, preheat the oven to 500°F.

Place each rack of ribs on a 2-foot-long sheet of aluminum foil. Rub with oil and sprinkle with salt, the herb sprigs, and garlic. Wrap the foil around each rack tightly and place in a roasting pan.

Roast the ribs for 30 minutes, then turn the oven to 250°F and cook until the ribs are fork-tender, about 1½ hours longer. Remove from the oven and carefully pierce the foil of each packet to let the hot air escape. Set the ribs aside until cool enough to handle, about 15 minutes. Remove the foil and discard the herb sprigs and garlic.

Turn your oven to broil. Liberally brush the meaty side of the ribs with half of the sauce and broil until the sauce is caramelized, 2 to 3 minutes. (If you don't have a built-in broiling element in your oven, then crank the oven to 500°F and roast the ribs until the sauce is hot and bubbling.)

Transfer the ribs to a platter and pass the remaining barbecue sauce at the table.

WHAT YOU NEED TO KNOW

In a nutshell: Paper napkins. Masses of them.

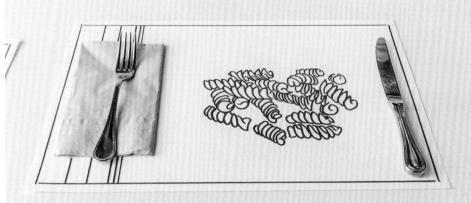

JON AND VINNY

Jon Shook and Vinny Dotolo are irrepressible in just about everything they do. Take a look at the mischief in their grins, the magnums of Les Grands Cru Classés in the back shop of their pizza parlor, the sticks of butter and pints of cream in their pasta sauce, the dreamscapes of bacon on their breakfast pizzas. Keen observers of their local habitat, they are masters of high-end low-brow, offering up guilty, carnivorous pleasures made with the true precision of schooled craftsmen.

PORK ADOBO

Adobo refers to the Philippine technique of marinating meat overnight, usually in a mixture of vinegar, soy sauce, garlic, bay leaves, and black pepper, and then transferring it to the stove to braise. Chef Marge Manzke takes it a step further and adds brown sugar, giving it a nod to Southern barbecue.

Manzke is from the Philippines, and her adobo is much loved in Los Angeles. Wes Avila learned to make this pork and now sells it wrapped in a tortilla out of his Guerrilla Taco truck. Highly recommended! The meat also makes for a great pulled pork sandwich or a quick meal if it's sitting on greens and topped with a poached egg. Or try it in sweet potato hash browns. In other words, options abound, which is why I cook an entire shoulder and turn it into a few meals.

MARINADE

4 cups soy sauce

1⅓ cups distilled white vinegar

1 (3-inch) piece ginger, peeled and finely chopped

3 garlic cloves, finely chopped

3 bay leaves, fresh or dried

15 black peppercorns

5 star anise pods

PORK

6 pounds bone-in pork shoulder or pork butt

Serves 6

ADOBO SAUCE

3 cups pork, beef or chicken stock

1 cup soy sauce

½ cup distilled white vinegar

2 tablespoons light or dark brown sugar

1 (2-inch) piece ginger, peeled and sliced

5 black peppercorns

¼ yellow or red onion, chopped

5 garlic cloves, chopped

3 star anise pods

2 bay leaves, fresh or dried

To make the marinade, combine all of the ingredients in a saucepan. Bring to a boil, then immediately remove from heat and let cool.

When the marinade is at a cool room temperature, pour it over the pork and let the pork marinate for 1 to 2 days in the fridge in a covered bowl or container.

Preheat the oven to 300°F. Remove the pork from the fridge and place the pork and its marinade in a lidded braising pan or Dutch oven. Bring the marinade to a simmer over medium-high heat. Transfer to the oven and cook, covered, for 4 hours, or until the meat is fork-tender. Another hour or so won't hurt. Just turn the oven down to 250°F until you are ready to use the pork.

Meanwhile, make the adobo sauce: Combine all of the ingredients in a saucepan and bring to a boil over high heat. Turn down the heat and cook at a lively simmer until the liquid is reduced by half, about 10 minutes. Remove from the heat and let the flavors infuse for half an hour or so. Strain through a fine-mesh sieve, discarding the solids and reserving the liquid.

Remove the pork from the oven and let cool. When cool enough to handle, pull the pork meat apart—it should naturally tear off into strips. To make pulled pork, you want strips that are roughly 2 inches long and ½ inch thick, but the point of this casual dish is that nothing need be too regular or uniform. The odd chunk that is larger or smaller is welcome. The pork can be served atop rice, hamburger buns, in burritos, mixed into hash browns and, in the following recipe, made into fried rice. Serve with the adobo sauce.

WHAT YOU NEED TO KNOW

Use leftovers in the adobo fried rice (facing page).

ADOBO FRIED RICE

Many people consider fried rice something you make with leftovers. Not my husband, John. Nor my son, Garrick. They consider this fried rice to more than justify marinating a shoulder of pork for twenty-four hours. And when it comes to Manzke's adobo, I won't argue.

3 tablespoons grapeseed oil

1½ cups cooked pork (such as Pork Adobo, facing page), shredded

pinch of minced garlic

¼ to ½ cup of adobo sauce (facing page), or to taste

3 cups cooked white jasmine rice

2 eggs

a few scallions, thinly sliced on the diagonal

a few paper-thin slices of Fresno chile (preferably pickled) or serrano chiles

salt, as needed

Serves 2

In a heavy skillet, heat the grapeseed oil until it is hot but not smoking. Add the pork and cook it about 1 minute, or until browned on all sides. Add the garlic followed by the adobo sauce and cook for 1 to 2 minutes to reduce the sauce a bit. Add the rice and fry it until hot, tossing continuously; you will know it's done when there's no liquid left in the pan and the rice is piping hot.

If you are adding the eggs to the rice, stir them in now and let them cook through. Otherwise, fry two eggs sunny-side up. Plate the fried rice, top with the fried eggs, and sprinkle with the scallions and chile. The adobo sauce is salty, but check the seasoning and salt the dish if needed.

WHAT YOU NEED TO KNOW

This is more a blueprint than a recipe. It makes about two servings, which works well in a 10-inch skillet or wok. It's hard to make fried rice for a crowd as you need room in the pan to toss the ingredients around. But it is so quick to make that a second batch is easily fried. As to the eggs, some people like their egg stirred into the rice as it is frying and others like their rice topped with a fried or poached egg. The choice is yours.

SPAGHETTI WITH MEATBALLS

When Australian-born Stone moved to Los Angeles in 2013, he was at once overwhelmed by the sun-ripened produce of Southern California and disheartened by the lack of good butcheries. He opened Gwen, a restaurant with an in-house meat shop, as much to fill an apparent need as to source his own meat, with an eye to both quality and provenance. The idea took hold and spots have opened up all over town with the same concept. But few chefs can match Stone's knowledge of meat. Here, in this classic meatball recipe, he ups the ante by using well-marbled, dry-aged Wagyu beef, which he combines with a smaller quantity of pork to round out the flavor. The tanginess of buttermilk and Pecorino Romano balance the nuttiness of the Parmesan, while the balsamic-laced pomodoro sauce teases with both sweet and sour notes.

MEATBALLS

¾ cup finely crumbled day-old bread (such as ciabatta)

1 cup buttermilk

1½ pounds well-marbled (not lean!) ground beef or ground dry-aged Wagyu beef

⅔ pound ground pork (20% fat; nothing less)

½ cup finely chopped flat-leaf parsley

½ cup grated Parmesan

⅔ cup grated Pecorino Romano

2 large garlic cloves, grated on a Microplane

1 to 1½ tablespoons kosher salt

1½ teaspoons chopped fresh oregano

½ teaspoon red pepper flakes

½ teaspoon ground fennel seeds

½ teaspoon black pepper

3 eggs

¼ cup olive oil

POMODORO SAUCE

3 tablespoons olive oil

1 small yellow onion, very thinly sliced

3 garlic cloves, finely chopped

kosher salt

1 teaspoon sugar

⅛ teaspoon cayenne pepper

1 (28-ounce) can whole peeled tomatoes (preferably organic San Marzano tomatoes), crushed by hand

2 tablespoons butter

1 tablespoon balsamic vinegar

black pepper

SPAGHETTI

1 pound spaghetti

salt and black pepper

grated Parmesan, for serving

Serves 4

To make the meatballs, combine the bread crumbs and buttermilk in a large bowl. Set aside for half an hour to let the bread crumbs absorb the liquid. Squeeze out any excess buttermilk from the bread crumbs and discard.

Using your hands, mash the bread crumbs. Add the beef, pork, parsley, Parmesan, Pecorino, garlic, kosher salt, oregano, pepper flakes, fennel seeds, and black pepper and mix thoroughly until blended; do not over-work it.

Whisk the eggs, then add to the meat. Using your hands, gently incorporate them into the meat. The mixture will be soft, which will ensure tender meat-balls. Form the mixture into 12 meatballs, each about 2½ inches in diameter.

Heat a large heavy skillet over medium heat. Pour in the olive oil. Working in batches, add the meatballs and cook, turning occasionally, for 12 minutes per batch, or until browned all over. Using a slotted spoon, transfer to a plate.

Meanwhile, bring a large pot of heavily salted water to a boil.

To make the pomodoro sauce, heat the olive oil in a wide pot over medium-low heat. Add the onion and garlic and sauté for 5 to 8 minutes, or until the onions have softened and become translucent. Stir in 2 tea-spoons kosher salt, the sugar, and cayenne and cook for another 2 minutes.

Add the tomatoes and simmer gently, stirring occa-sionally, for 15 minutes. Whisk in the butter and vinegar. Season with salt and pepper.

Add the meatballs and cook at a bare simmer for 10 minutes, or until the meatballs are cooked through, with no sign of pink.

While the meatballs are cooking, make the spaghetti. Add the pasta to the boiling water and cook until al dente, then drain it. Toss the spaghetti with the pomo-doro sauce and serve, topping each serving with three meatballs, a grinding of salt and pepper, and a spoonful or two of Parmesan.

WHAT YOU NEED TO KNOW

If you can't locate Wagyu beef, simply use well-marbled beef. Neither meat should be lean—that's the key. If your Pecorino is extremely salty, you will need less salt, so do taste the cheese before making the meatballs.

CHINOIS LAMB CHOPS WITH CILANTRO MINT VINAIGRETTE

Wolfgang Puck's Chinois chicken salad was one of the most influential recipes of the 1980s, catapulting Puck into national celebrity. His Santa Monica restaurant, Chinois on Main, was synonymous with an era of Californian fusion food that most often paired French technique with Asian ingredients. That his Chinois salads remain among the most copied recipes is a testament to a simple fact: they are good. At Spago, he has adapted those Chinois flavors to lamb, which he serves hot on a bed of herb sauce and alongside a salad of tender greens. It is a bite of Los Angeles.

16 lamb chops

salt and freshly ground pepper

MARINADE

1 cup soy sauce

1 cup mirin

½ cup chopped scallions

1 tablespoon red pepper flakes

2 or 3 garlic cloves, finely chopped

SAUCE

¼ cup coarsely chopped fresh mint

¼ cup coarsely chopped fresh cilantro

¼ cup coarsely chopped fresh parsley

½ cup peanut oil

½ cup rice vinegar

2 egg yolks (optional)

chile oil, to taste (optional)

salt and black pepper

VINAIGRETTE

½ cup peanut oil

¼ cup rice vinegar

1 teaspoon white miso

1 teaspoon finely chopped fresh ginger

salt and black pepper

TO SERVE

2 or 3 heads tender young lettuce, such as butterhead or mâche, leaves separated

To make the marinade, mix together all of the ingredients in a bowl.

Put the lamb chops in a baking dish or resealable plastic bag. Pour the marinade over the lamb chops and set aside for 30 minutes at room temperature. While the lamb marinates, make the sauce and vinaigrette.

To make the sauce, combine all of the ingredients, except the salt and pepper, in a blender and purée until smooth. Season with salt and pepper to taste. Transfer to a pitcher or bowl.

To make the vinaigrette, whisk together all of the ingredients, except the salt and pepper, in a bowl. Season with salt and pepper to taste.

Remove the chops from the marinade and season with salt and pepper. Sauté them in a pan over high heat for about 2 minutes on each side, or until pink in the center. Cook the chops in several batches if necessary, but don't crowd the pan.

Toss the salad greens with enough of the vinaigrette to coat them lightly. Serve the lamb chops on a bed of sauce next to the salad and pass around additional sauce at the table for anyone who might want some.

WHAT YOU NEED TO KNOW

If serving these chops to anyone who should not eat raw eggs, simply omit the sauce and shower the lamb with picked leaves of cilantro, mint, and parsley.

Serves 4

Bryant Ng of Cassia, Santa Monica

SPICY LAMB BREAST

Spicy and fiery, this is a boldly flavored lamb. Rice is your friend here, to temper the heat and soak up the sauce. And so is cold beer. I like to follow this dish with either the Kaffir Lime Pudding (page 206) or the Meyer Lemon–Olive Oil Ice Cream (page 187) to cool the palate.

RUB

½ cup cumin seeds, toasted

¼ cup coriander seeds, toasted

½ cup Sichuan peppercorns, toasted

¼ cup sesame seeds

¼ cup sugar

¼ cup garlic powder

3 tablespoons spicy chile powder (preferably Vietnamese)

2 tablespoons anchovy salt (preferably Red Boat)

2 tablespoons salt

LAMB

2 lamb breasts (about 2½ pounds each)

2 tablespoons soy sauce

4 onions, cut into ½-inch slices

½ cup Sichuan chile oil or sambal oelek

2 tablespoons Shaoxing wine

1 tablespoon toasted sesame oil

1 tablespoon low-sodium soy sauce

WHITE SAUCE

¼ cup water

1 tablespoon Chinese sesame paste or tahini

1 tablespoon freshly squeezed lemon juice

½ teaspoon ground cardamom

¾ teaspoon pepper

salt

1 cup mayonnaise

TO SERVE

grilled onions (optional)

cooked jasmine rice

sambal oelek or Sichuan chile oil, to taste

lemon wedges

1 bunch cilantro

Serves 4 to 6

To make the rub, grind the toasted cumin, coriander seeds, and peppercorns in a coffee or spice grinder, then combine with the remaining ingredients.

To make the lamb, rub the soy sauce into the lamb breasts, then season liberally with half of the rub, patting it on to adhere. Reserve the remaining rub for the onions. Cover with plastic wrap and refrigerate overnight.

The following day, remove the lamb from the fridge and bring to room temperature. Preheat the oven to 250°F.

Sear the lamb in a lightly oiled skillet or on a grill to brown it.

In a bowl, toss the onions with the remaining lamb rub, the chile oil, Shaoxing wine, sesame oil, and low-sodium soy sauce. Place the onions in the bottom of a roasting pan. Place the lamb breasts on top of the onions. Cover the lamb with a sheet of aluminum foil, and then tightly cover with a second layer of foil. Cook for 2½ or 3 hours, or until tender. Transfer the lamb to a platter or cutting board to rest. Drain the onions and set aside to cool.

To make the white sauce, whisk together the water, sesame paste, lemon juice, cardamom, pepper, and salt to taste in a bowl until the sesame paste is smooth and integrated, then fold in the mayonnaise.

Serve the lamb, carved, with the onions (if using), cooked white rice, a spoonful of sambal oelek, a squeeze of lemon, a shower of cilantro leaves, and the white sauce on the side.

WHAT YOU NEED TO KNOW

Lamb breast is an inexpensive cut of meat that is served on the bone and is a little fattier than lamb chops. It yields beautifully to low-temperature roasting, but benefits from either an initial sear or a few minutes under a broiler before roasting. The lamb needs to cure in a dry rub overnight, so plan accordingly.

Suzanne Goin of A. O. C., Melrose

LAMB MEATBALLS, SPICED TOMATO SAUCE, MINT, AND FETA

Goin's food is bountiful and generous. Her inspiration lies in the rustic cuisines of the Mediterranean, but the heartiness of her presentation belies the intuitive and nuanced refinement of a master. Her cooking satisfies at every level. Disparate textures keep the palate interested, intriguing notes of sweet and sour keep it guessing, and an impeccable balance of bright herbaceous notes spin it Californian. We all have foods we crave—perhaps it's a hankering for steak or the memory of a chocolate mousse—but Goin's food, in itself, is one that spurs yearning in me. These cumin- and cinnamon-scented meatballs are everything I love about her cooking in one spicy little ball. Cook them and you'll see why.

SPICED TOMATO SAUCE

3 cups canned tomatoes (preferably San Marzano)

½ teaspoon cumin seeds

3 tablespoons olive oil

1 small sprig rosemary

1 chile de arbol, crushed

1 cup diced yellow or red onion

1 teaspoon fresh thyme leaves

pinch of cumin

pinch of ground cinnamon

pinch of cayenne pepper

1 bay leaf (preferably fresh)

½ teaspoon sugar

¼ cup freshly squeezed orange juice, plus 3-inch strip of orange zest

kosher salt and black pepper

MEATBALLS

¾ cup finely diced onion

¼ cup heavy cream

2 extra-large egg yolks

1 teaspoon ground cumin

1 teaspoon ground Aleppo pepper

½ teaspoon ground cinnamon

pinch of cayenne pepper

2 pounds ground lamb

kosher salt and black pepper

1 cup fresh bread crumbs

¼ cup chopped fresh flat-leaf parsley

¼ cup olive oil

TO SERVE

4 ounces feta cheese, crumbled

2 tablespoons sliced fresh mint

To make the spiced tomato sauce, pass the tomatoes through a food mill or pulse in a food processor until broken up.

Toast the cumin seeds for a few minutes in a small pan over medium heat, until fragrant and lightly browned. Let cool for a few minutes, then either pound them finely with a mortar and pestle or blitz in a coffee or spice grinder.

Heat a medium saucepan over medium-high heat for 1 minute. Swirl in the olive oil, add the rosemary and chile, and heat for another minute. Add the onion, thyme, cumin, cinnamon, cayenne, and bay leaf and sauté for 5 to 6 minutes, or until the onion is translucent. Add the tomatoes, sugar, orange juice and zest, a heaping ½ teaspoon salt, and pepper to taste. Cook for 8 to 10 minutes over medium-low heat, until the sauce is reduced by one-third.

To make the meatballs, in a large bowl, mix together the onion, cream, egg yolks, cumin, Aleppo pepper, cinnamon, and cayenne. Add the lamb and season evenly with 2½ teaspoons kosher salt and lots of black pepper. Add the bread crumbs and parsley. This is the moment to get in there with your hands and really work the ingredients together with a thorough, but light touch. Shape the meat into small balls, just slightly larger than golf balls.

Preheat the oven to 400°F. Pour the tomato sauce into a large oven-to-table baking dish.

Heat two large sauté pans over high heat for 2 minutes. Swirl 2 tablespoons of the oil in each pan and wait a minute. Place the meatballs carefully in the pans and cook for a few minutes, until the bottoms are nicely browned. Turn the meatballs over and continue cooking on all sides until they are evenly colored. Transfer the meatballs to the baking dish, placing them ½ inch apart.

Bake for 15 to 20 minutes, until the sauce is bubbling and the meatballs are just cooked through. Top the meatballs with crumbled feta and a shower of mint.

Serves 4

SAUCES, SIDES, AND SALSA

BEET MUHAMMARA

This is a riff on Syrian muhammara, made with raw beets instead of the customary roasted peppers. Serve it as a dip alongside crudités and a smear of labneh or spread it on a plate that is piled high with roasted vegetables and a generous drizzle of olive oil. It's wonderful with roasted beets, shaved cucumbers, and garlicky yogurt. Perhaps add a bright, lemony salad of arugula, scallions, and dill. Needless to say, it sports the vibrant purple of its star ingredient.

2½ cups peeled, cubed raw beets

1¾ cups toasted walnuts

2 or 3 garlic cloves, peeled

2¼ teaspoons ground cumin

2 tablespoons freshly squeezed lemon juice, plus more to taste

2½ heaping teaspoons Urfa Biber chile flakes

2½ tablespoons pomegranate molasses

1¼ teaspoons Maldon sea salt, plus more to taste

lots of good olive oil, for blending

Makes 4 cups

Toss everything but the olive oil into a food processor and blitz until the ingredients are broken down. With the motor running, drizzle in the olive oil until the mixture is thick and emulsified. It might take awhile to break down the beets, but keep at it! Season to taste with additional sea salt and lemon juice. The finished muhammara should have a coarse but even texture. Store in a sealed glass jar in the fridge for up to 3 days.

WHAT YOU NEED TO KNOW

Urfa Biber chile is easily found online. It is sometimes called Isot chile and is wonderfully dark and smoky. Wear gloves when peeling beets or your fingers will turn pink!

BOTANICA

Botanica is, in a word, pretty. And by that, I mean that the sun-filled airy space, the artful plates of colorful vegetables with their garlands of tiny white cilantro flowers and showering of yellow nasturtiums, their lovingly crafted ceramics, and seemingly home-baked cookies and cakes, all combine and conspire to please in the loveliest way. This is that spot we all wish we had within a stone's throw of our homes or offices. That the food is healthy, vegetable-focused, fresh, seasonal, and delicious only adds to the appeal. At the heart of Botanica are two great friends, chefs and co-owners, Emily Fiffer and Heather Sperling. Botanica was conceived in friendship and, in every detail, embodies that spirit of warmth and ease.

Travis Lett of Gjelina, Venice Beach

CARROT TOP PISTOU

Dollop this unusual pistou onto roasted carrots for a tasty reunion of carrot and top or spread it onto a slab of grilled bread and top with chèvre or ricotta and a few shavings of raw carrot.

2 tablespoons pepitas

¼ teaspoon coriander seeds

½ cup carrot tops

½ cup fresh flat-leaf parsley leaves

½ shallot, peeled and minced

zest of 1 orange

zest of 1 lemon

2 garlic cloves

1 cup olive oil

kosher salt

2 tablespoons grated Pecorino Romano

1 tablespoon balsamic vinegar

juice of ½ lemon

Makes 1 cup

In a small, dry frying pan over medium heat, toast the pepitas until just fragrant and beginning to brown, 3 to 5 minutes. Remove from the pan and set aside.

In the same pan, toast the coriander seeds over medium heat until just fragrant and beginning to brown, 3 to 5 minutes. Remove from the heat and let cool before grinding to a fine powder in a coffee or spice grinder.

Finely chop the carrot tops and parsley. Combine with the shallot, zests, and ground coriander. Using a Microplane, grate the garlic into the mixture, then stir in the olive oil. Season with salt to taste. Set aside to let the flavors mingle for half an hour.

At this point, the mixture may be stored in the fridge in an airtight container for a few days. Before serving, bring to room temperature, then stir in the Pecorino, pepitas, vinegar, and lemon juice.

WHAT YOU NEED TO KNOW

Buy carrots with their green tops still attached. Discard any of the green tops that are old and tough. The beauty of this dish lies in choosing young, tender tops.

BROCCOLI RABE PESTO

Chef Curtis Stone lavishes this pesto on rolls when making meatball subs. For a vegetarian option, dollop it onto grilled, olive oil–brushed slabs of bread. Or serve a few spoonfuls alongside scrambled eggs. The gentleness of the eggs will balance the appealing bitterness of this pesto.

Combine the broccoli rabe, peppadews, pickle brine, garlic, pepper flakes, and Parmesan in a food processor. With the processor running, slowly pour in the oil until blended. Season to taste. This may be made 1 day in advance and kept in a sealed glass jar in the refrigerator. Return to room temperature before using.

1 bunch broccoli rabe, blanched and coarsely chopped

⅓ cup jarred pickled peppadew peppers

¼ cup peppadew pickle brine from the jar

2 garlic cloves, peeled

1 teaspoon red pepper flakes

¾ cup grated Parmesan

⅓ cup olive oil

sea salt, to taste

Makes about 2 cups

David LeFevre of Manhattan Beach Post, Manhattan Beach

GREEN OLIVE PESTO

Try this with mozzarella, burrata, chèvre or fresh feta. Or smear on grilled bread, topped with a few roasted peppers or tomatoes.

2 cups pitted Castelvetrano olives

½ cup pine nuts

2 cups fresh flat-leaf parsley leaves

½ cup fresh basil leaves

¼ red onion

zest and juice of 1 lemon

1 garlic clove, halved

1 teaspoon red pepper flakes

⅔ cup olive oil

In a food processor, combine all of the ingredients excluding the olive oil. Pulse to chop and incorporate. Slowly drizzle in the olive oil and pulse until the pesto is coarse but integrated. This may be made 1 day in advance and kept in a sealed glass jar in the refrigerator. Return to room temperature before using.

Makes about 4 cups

GREEN HARISSA

Use this wonder sauce on grilled fish, shrimp, chicken, and vegetables or dolloped on couscous. Better yet, scoop it up with warm pita or just a spoon.

¼ teaspoon cumin seeds

½ teaspoon coriander seeds

2 tablespoons olive oil

5 tomatillos, husked and halved

3 jalapeño chiles, coarsely chopped

2 shallots, coarsely chopped

2 garlic cloves, sliced

kosher salt and pepper

½ packed cup fresh cilantro leaves

½ packed cup fresh flat-leaf parsley leaves

2 tablespoons freshly squeezed lime juice

1 tablespoon white wine vinegar

Makes 1½ cups

In a small, dry frying pan over medium heat, toast the cumin and coriander seeds just until fragrant and beginning to brown, about 3 minutes. Remove from the heat and let cool before grinding to a powder in a spice grinder.

In the same frying pan, warm the olive oil over medium-high heat until hot but not smoking. Add the tomatillos, jalapeños, shallots, and garlic to the pan and cook until the shallots are translucent and the jalapeños are tender, 6 to 8 minutes. Season with salt and pepper. Remove from the heat and let cool for about 10 minutes.

In a food processor, process the cooled tomatillo mixture with the cilantro, parsley, and the ground cumin and coriander until smooth.

You may make the harissa 1 day in advance up until this point. Simply refrigerate in a sealed glass jar. Return to room temperature before proceeding.

Stir in the lime juice and vinegar. Taste and adjust the seasoning before serving.

HARISSA

This is the harissa that chef Miriello uses when making Harissa Chicken with Stewed Chickpeas and Tzatziki (page 140) but it is also simply a great homemade harissa to keep on hand in the fridge and serve with anything from a traditional couscous to a simple plate of roasted carrots. Try a spoonful on grain bowls, soups, grilled bread, and scrambled eggs. The harissa will keep for two weeks, but note that its potency will increase over time, as garlic has a tendency to grow more potent and, unfortunately, pungent.

2 large yellow onions, coarsely chopped

2 large carrots, peeled and coarsely chopped

8 garlic cloves, coarsely chopped

olive oil, as needed

1 tablespoon cumin seeds

1 tablespoon coriander seeds

⅓ cup tomato paste

4 cups guajillo chiles, stemmed and seeded

¼ cup chiles de arbol, stemmed and seeded

water, as needed

zest of 1 preserved lemon

juice of 1 fresh lemon, plus more to taste

¼ cup kosher salt

Makes roughly 4 cups

Place a large cast-iron or other wide, heavy skillet over high heat. Char the onions, carrots, and garlic. Don't be afraid—you want a real char here, so embrace the burn. The vegetables should be blackened in places. After 5 minutes, add a touch of olive oil to the pan and continue to char.

Add the cumin and coriander and toast to release their aromas. Add the tomato paste and let it caramelize for 1 minute without stirring. Add the guajillo and arbol chiles, then stir and add just enough water to cover the ingredients. Deglaze the pan, stirring up all of the good char off the bottom, and cook until most of the water evaporates. Repeat, adding more water, and cooking it off again. Continue to repeat this process for half an hour.

Add the preserved lemon zest, the lemon juice, and gradually, the kosher salt; you may not need all of it. Using a slotted spoon, transfer the solids to a Vitamix or another high-powered blender. Add cooking liquid as needed as you blend to form a paste. Season with additional salt and lemon juice, to taste.

If not using immediately, store in a covered jar in the fridge for up to 1 week. Any longer and the garlic will become too pungent. Bring to room temperature and stir before use.

WHAT YOU NEED TO KNOW

This is hot! If you prefer less heat, reduce the quantity of chiles de arbol by half. If you swing fiery, don't discard the seeds. Seeds contain the real heat in a pepper.

Jaime Martin del Campo and Ramiro Arvizu of La Casita Mexicana, Bell

PEPITAS AND PEANUT SALSA

The peanuts here are surprising at first bite but offer a smooth sweetness to counter the heat of the chiles. Serve with tortilla chips or dollop onto enchiladas.

1 cup plus 2 tablespoons olive oil

3 serrano chiles, seeded, stemmed and finely chopped

4 chiles de arbol, seeded

¼ cup peeled shelled peanuts

¼ cup pepitas

½ teaspoon salt

Makes 1½ cups

Heat 2 tablespoons of the olive oil in a skillet over medium heat. Add the serranos and cook until lightly browned. Add the chiles de arbol and cook until they, too, are lightly browned. Transfer the chiles to a paper towel–lined plate to remove excess oil.

In a clean pan, toast the peanuts and pepitas (pumpkin seeds) until golden and fragrant, 3 to 5 minutes. Remove from the heat and let cool for 10 minutes.

Grind all of the ingredients in a *molcajete* or pulse in a food processor or blender until nearly smooth. Pour in the remaining 1 cup olive oil little by little and mix into a thick sauce. Season with the salt. This may be stored in a sealed glass jar in the refrigerator for up to 3 days.

FROZEN TREATS AND HOT SAUCES

Jessica Mortarotti and Zachary Cox of Carmela Ice Cream, Pasadena

CRANBERRY THYME SORBET

This is as strikingly beautiful as it is delicious. Here, tart cranberries give a cool pucker against thyme's savory, herbal backdrop. Pair it with the Spiced Apple Sorbet (page 191) or let it stand alone in all its ruby red glory.

2 cups cranberries, fresh or frozen and thawed

1¾ cups sugar

2 cups water

½ packed cup thyme sprigs

2 tablespoons grated orange zest

¾ cup freshly squeezed orange juice

Makes about 1 quart

Pulse the cranberries in a food processor a few times to coarsely break them. Transfer the cranberries to a container and toss them with the sugar. Refrigerate the macerating berries overnight.

In a large pot, combine the macerated cranberries, the water, thyme sprigs, and orange zest and bring to a boil over medium heat. Lower the heat and simmer for 10 minutes. Remove from the heat and let sit 30 minutes.

Prepare an ice bath. Strain the cranberry mixture through a fine-mesh sieve into a metal bowl set in the ice bath. Once cold, whisk in the orange juice. Discard any remaining solids.

Churn in an ice cream machine according to the manufacturer's instructions and freeze in airtight containers for at least 2 hours before serving.

Kumi Takahashi of Gresescent Ice Cream, Downtown Arts District

BLACKBERRY MINT MOJITO ICE CREAM

A decidedly adult ice cream. Think of this as a mojito given a creamy, cool spin and a swirl of homemade blackberry lime jam. Try it with a slice of coconut layer cake or simply served in a coupe glass with a small spoon and a shortbread cookie.

BLACKBERRY LIME JAM

4 cups fresh blackberries

½ cup sugar

2½ tablespoons corn syrup

¼ cup freshly squeezed lime juice

1½ tablespoons pectin

ICE CREAM BASE

1½ cups heavy cream

1½ cups whole milk

1 packed cup fresh mint leaves

2 tablespoons grated lime zest

⅓ cup granulated sugar

¼ cup turbinado sugar

4 egg yolks

1 tablespoon coconut rum

2 tablespoons white rum

Makes 1 quart

WHAT YOU NEED TO KNOW

You will need pectin to make the blackberry jam. Pectin accelerates the process of thickening fruit into a jammy consistency. It's easily found in most grocery shops. Alternatively, substitute a good store-bought blackberry jam.

Homemade ice cream lasts roughly one month in the freezer if well sealed. Any longer than that and you may find it has crystallized and lost its smooth texture.

To make the jam, combine the berries, ¼ cup of the sugar, the corn syrup, and the lime juice in a medium pot and bring to a simmer over low heat, gently crushing the berries with a wooden spoon as you stir.

Whisk the remaining ¼ cup sugar and pectin together in a bowl and, continuing to whisk, sprinkle into the simmering jam. Continue to cook the jam until it boils and activates the pectin. This will thicken the jam.

Pour the jam into a container and lay plastic wrap over the surface to prevent a skin from forming. Refrigerate until chilled or up to several days.

To make the ice cream base, combine the cream, milk, mint and lime zest in a medium saucepan and cook over low heat, whisking occasionally, until it just begins to simmer. Remove from the heat and let steep for 30 minutes.

Pick out and discard the mint leaves. Stir in the sugars and return the mixture to a simmer over low heat, stirring to dissolve the sugars.

In a separate bowl, whisk the egg yolks. Once the cream mixture is at a simmer, slowly pour about a third of it into the eggs, while whisking constantly. Then pour the combined mixture back into the saucepan and continue to whisk. Return the mixture to a simmer and continue to cook for about 4 minutes, or until it has thickened enough to coat the back of a spoon.

Prepare an ice bath. Strain the custard through a fine-mesh sieve into a metal bowl set in the ice bath. Add the rums and whisk occasionally until thoroughly chilled.

Churn in an ice cream machine according to the manufacturer's instructions. Transfer the ice cream to a bowl and fold in all of the blackberry jam by hand to create ribbons of jam throughout. Freeze in airtight containers for at least 2 hours before serving.

Meadow Ramsey of Kismet, Los Feliz

BUCKWHEAT ICE CREAM

This is a subtle, earthy ice cream that pairs beautifully with fruit crisps and cobblers. I serve it when I want to avoid the familiar sweetness of vanilla or when I want to accentuate the flavor of seeds, grains, and nuts in a cake or cookie. Try it with the Toasted Sesame Cake (page 212), the Pistachio Semolina Cake (page 218), or topped with the Vegan, Dairy-Free Date Caramel (page 193).

BUCKWHEAT MILK

1¼ cup buckwheat groats

6 cups whole milk

ICE CREAM BASE

4 cups buckwheat milk

1¼ cups heavy cream

1¼ cups sugar

8 egg yolks

¾ teaspoon salt

Makes about 1½ quarts

To make the buckwheat milk, combine the buckwheat groats and milk in a large pot. Cook over medium heat, whisking occasionally, until it just begins to simmer. Remove from the heat and let steep for 30 minutes at room temperature. Strain the milk through a fine-mesh sieve and discard the groats, or reserve to eat for breakfast.

To make the ice cream base, combine 4 cups of the buckwheat milk, the cream, and 1 cup of the sugar in a large pot and bring almost to a simmer over medium-low heat, whisking occasionally. (Save or discard the remaining milk.)

Meanwhile, whisk the egg yolks with the remaining ¼ cup sugar and the salt in a bowl.

Once the milk mixture is nearly at a simmer, slowly pour about a third of it into the yolks, while whisking constantly. Continue to whisk for 20 seconds or so, then pour the combined mixture back into the saucepan and continue to whisk. Return the mixture to a simmer and continue to cook for about 4 minutes, or until it has thickened enough to coat the back of a spoon.

Prepare an ice bath. Strain the custard through a fine-mesh sieve into a metal bowl set in the ice bath and whisk occasionally until thoroughly chilled.

Churn in an ice cream machine according to the manufacturer's instructions. Freeze in airtight containers for at least 2 hours before serving.

WHAT YOU NEED TO KNOW

You really do need buckwheat groats to make this. Using buckwheat flour instead may be tempting but, alas, won't work in this recipe. Groats are easily found in health food stores and online. The good news is that making this ice cream will give you cooked groats for breakfast. Just reheat them with a bit of milk and a swirl of maple syrup.

CANDIED CLEMENTINE AND VANILLA BEAN ICE CREAM

This winner of an ice cream has it all—sticky-sweet candied clementines and a rich smooth vanilla base. Consider it the grown-up version of a Creamsicle.

CANDIED CLEMENTINES

4 clementines

¼ teaspoon salt

8 cups water

2 cups sugar

¼ cup light corn syrup

ICE CREAM BASE

1⅓ cups whole milk

1⅓ cups heavy cream

1 vanilla bean, split lengthwise

1 teaspoon vanilla extract

2 tablespoons light corn syrup

½ cup sugar

2 tablespoons nonfat dry milk powder

¼ teaspoon xanthan gum

Makes 1 quart

To candy the clementines, pierce each one a dozen or so times with a safety pin or sewing needle.

In a small pot, combine the clementines and salt. Add 4 cups of the water and bring to a boil. Turn the heat to low and simmer for 5 minutes. Remove from the heat, drain the clementines, and set aside.

In the same pot, combine the sugar, corn syrup, and 4 more cups of the water. Bring to a boil and cook, stirring, until the sugar has completely dissolved. Add the clementines, turn the heat to medium, and simmer for 10 minutes. Remove from the heat and set aside at room temperature overnight.

On the second day, return the pot to medium heat and simmer for 10 minutes. Remove from the heat and set aside at room temperature overnight.

On the third day, repeat.

On the fourth day, return the pot to medium heat, but this time, simmer the clementines until the syrup reaches 230°F on a candy thermometer. Remove from the heat and let the clementines cool to room temperature. With a slotted spoon, transfer the clementines to a cutting board and finely chop them. Return the clementines to their syrup and set aside for an hour or so to allow the fruit to absorb any excess liquid.

To make the ice cream base, combine the milk, cream, vanilla bean, extract, corn syrup, and sugar in a large pot and bring almost to a simmer over medium-low heat, whisking occasionally.

Meanwhile, combine the dry milk powder and xanthan gum in a small bowl. Slowly pour this into the cream mixture, whisking vigorously as you pour to keep the mixture from clumping.

Continue to cook, whisking occasionally, for about 4 minutes, until it has thickened enough to coat the back of a spoon.

Prepare an ice bath. Strain the custard through a fine-mesh sieve into a metal bowl set in the ice bath and whisk occasionally until thoroughly chilled.

Churn in an ice cream machine according to the manufacturer's instructions. Drain the clementines, discarding any excess liquid. When the ice cream is done, add the chopped clementines and turn the machine back on just long enough to incorporate them. Freeze in airtight containers for at least 2 hours before serving.

WHAT YOU NEED TO KNOW

Plan ahead! The clementines take four effortless days to candy. My advice is to double the batch of clementines as they are irresistible to anyone who might happen through the kitchen. They're fabulous on yogurt—and with anything chocolate. Dry milk powder and xanthan gum are easily purchased online. Xanthan gum is both a thickening agent and a stabilizer.

Jessica Mortarotti and Zachary Cox of Carmela Ice Cream, Pasadena

NUTMEG ICE CREAM

When I was little, my father used to bring me hot milk with nutmeg when I couldn't sleep or woke from a bad dream. The milk would make me sleepy and the nutmeg would hover warmly in my mouth with its sweet, woody notes. No wonder, then, that I ordered this ice cream as soon as I spotted it on the menu. Evocative and complex enough to serve alone, it is also gently powerful enough to pair with warm apple pie, Indian pudding, or all manner of cobblers and cakes. It won't put you to sleep, but will it jolt you awake like so many ice creams. It's cold and warm, familiar and exotic, and altogether a lovely, mellow way to end dinner.

1½ cups whole milk

1½ cups heavy cream

1 cup sugar

2 tablespoons freshly grated nutmeg

1 vanilla bean, split lengthwise

4 egg yolks

Makes 1 quart

In a large pot, combine the milk, cream, sugar, nutmeg, and vanilla bean and bring almost to a simmer over low heat, whisking occasionally.

Meanwhile, in a bowl, lightly whisk the egg yolks to break them up rather than froth them.

Once the cream mixture is nearly at a simmer, slowly pour about a third of it into the egg yolks, whisking constantly. Then pour the combined mixture back into the saucepan and continue to whisk. Return the mixture to a simmer and continue to cook for about 4 minutes, until it has thickened enough to coat the back of a spoon.

Prepare an ice bath. Strain the custard through a fine-mesh sieve into a metal bowl set in the ice bath and whisk occasionally until thoroughly chilled.

Churn in an ice cream machine according to the manufacturer's instructions. Freeze in airtight containers for at least 2 hours before serving.

WHAT YOU NEED TO KNOW

Nutmeg loses its flavor quite quickly once ground, so use fresh nutmeg and grate it on a Microplane or in a coffee grinder. Add a few scoops to cold chai tea and blend for a fabulous chai milk shake.

Tyler Malek of Salt and Straw, Hancock Park

LAVENDER ICE CREAM

Honeyed and floral, this beauty of an ice cream deserves a solo performance. Serve without adornment.

ICE CREAM BASE

½ cup sugar

2 tablespoons nonfat dry milk powder

¼ teaspoon xanthan gum

1⅓ cups whole milk

2 tablespoons light corn syrup

1⅓ cups heavy cream

LAVENDER SYRUP

¾ cup water

¼ cup wildflower honey

½ cup dry lavender petals

⅛ to ¼ teaspoon natural purple food coloring (optional)

Makes 1 quart

WHAT YOU NEED TO KNOW

If you want this ice cream to be the color of lavender, you need to add food coloring. To make your own natural dye, simply bring ½ cup blueberries or blackberries and 2 tablespoons water to a simmer over medium heat and cook for 5 minutes. Mash the berries with the back of a slotted spoon and let sit at room temperature to cool, about 15 minutes. Strain and discard the solids. Any remaining coloring may be frozen for later use. It also makes for a lovely-hued cupcake frosting.

To make the ice cream base, stir together the sugar, dry milk powder, and xanthan gum in a small bowl. Combine the milk and corn syrup in a medium pot and add the sugar mixture, whisking vigorously until smooth. Bring almost to a simmer over medium heat, whisking occasionally to dissolve the sugar, about 3 minutes. When it has almost reached a simmer, remove the pot from the heat and stir in the heavy cream.

Transfer this to an airtight container and refrigerate until thoroughly chilled, at least 4 hours and up to 24 hours.

To make the lavender syrup, combine the water and honey in a small saucepan and cook over medium heat. Once it starts to boil, remove the saucepan from the heat and add the lavender. Set aside to steep for at least 4 hours and up to 12 hours.

Strain and discard the solids. The lavender syrup can be used immediately or be refrigerated, covered, for up to 2 weeks.

To make the ice cream, combine ¾ cup of the lavender syrup, 3 cups of the ice cream base, and the food coloring, if using, in a bowl and whisk to thoroughly blend in the color.

Churn in an ice cream machine according to the manufacturer's instructions. Freeze in an airtight container for at least 2 hours before serving. This ice cream is also delicious soft serve. To prepare it this way, simply set the machine to churn to soft serve or remove the ice cream from the machine after half an hour.

FROZEN STRAWBERRY COCONUT ICE CREAM

This is not technically a sorbet, gelato, or ice cream, although, thanks to the coconut cream, it has the smooth texture of a gelato. It takes five minutes to make and is as healthy as a smoothie.

1 pound frozen strawberries

⅓ cup coconut cream, cold (from a 5.4-ounce can)

¼ cup honey

1 to 1½ teaspoons rose water, or to taste (optional)

Makes 1 pint

Combine all of the ingredients in a Vitamix or other high-powered blender—anything less powerful and you may need to use halved strawberries that are ever so slightly thawed.

Aggressively blend the mixture until the berries are completely broken down and pureed, 3 to 5 minutes. You'll need to stop a few times to shift the berries around and to push the ingredients down. The final result should have a smooth, whipped consistency. Serve immediately. This cream does not hold its texture if stored in the freezer.

WHAT YOU NEED TO KNOW

If it's strawberry season, trim, wash, pat dry, and halve a basket of berries, freeze them in a single layer so that they don't stick together, and proceed with the recipe. Any other time of year, simply use good frozen berries from the supermarket. Just make sure to break apart any that have stuck together or your blender will revolt. You may use 1 tablespoon of crème de framboise in place of the rose water. Be aware that brands of rose water vary in intensity. Taste as you add.

Jessica Mortarotti and Zachary Cox of Carmela Ice Cream, Pasadena

MEYER LEMON–OLIVE OIL ICE CREAM

It's hard to imagine an ice cream more Southern Californian than this one. Around Thanksgiving, the Meyer lemon trees in Los Angeles start bearing their fruit. Said to be a cross between a lemon and a mandarin orange, the Meyer lemon is just sweet enough to use in abundance, making it a favorite among chefs. Here, a good olive oil rounds out its tartness and gives it a silky texture. This is a perfect end to a spicy or rich meal, as the citrus will refresh and the cool creaminess will soothe. Serve with a simple shortbread cookie or a slice of olive oil cake.

1½ cups whole milk	4 egg yolks
1½ cups heavy cream	½ teaspoon salt
1 cup sugar	1 tablespoon olive oil
2 packed tablespoons grated Meyer lemon zest	2 tablespoons freshly squeezed Meyer lemon juice

Makes about 1 quart

In a large pot, combine the milk, cream, sugar, and lemon zest and bring almost to a simmer over low heat, whisking occasionally.

Meanwhile, in a bowl, lightly whisk the egg yolks to break them up rather than froth them. Whisk in the salt.

Once the cream mixture is nearly at a simmer, slowly pour about a third of it into the egg yolks, while whisking constantly. Then pour the combined mixture back into the saucepan and continue to whisk. Return the mixture to a simmer and continue to cook for about 4 minutes, until it has thickened enough to coat the back of a spoon.

Prepare an ice bath. Strain the custard through a fine-mesh sieve into a metal bowl set in the ice bath and whisk occasionally until thoroughly chilled. Add the olive oil and lemon juice to the custard, whisking to emulsify.

Churn in an ice cream machine according to the manufacturer's instructions. Freeze in airtight containers for 1 to 2 hours before serving.

WHAT YOU NEED TO KNOW

Use a really good, slightly fruity extra-virgin olive oil here. And if you are as crazy for Meyer lemons as I am, increase the amount of zest to 3 tablespoons. This ice cream is at its very best freshly churned and frozen. Remove from the freezer 5 minutes before serving to soften it a touch.

CARMELA ICE CREAM CO.

When Jessica Mortarotti and Zachary Cox started
Carmela Ice Cream Co. in 2007, neither knew how to
make ice cream, let alone how to run a business. It was a
gutsy, if not downright crazy, move, propelled by a desire
to celebrate the produce and dairy they found at farmers'
markets. The couple's first flavor was Rose and featured
local Pasadena roses. That might not be so radical today,
but twelve years ago the artisan ice cream movement
had barely begun, and the floral notes of the Middle East
were not yet popular among Los Angeles chefs. Brown
Butter Sage, Rosemary Pignoli, Lemon Basil—these
esoteric ice cream pairings put Carmela on the map, and
the couple now has three brick-and-mortar locations
and a truck for those very farmers' markets that inspired
what, in hindsight, was not such a crazy idea after all.

Sahar Shomali of Lucques, Melrose

CARDAMOM ICE CREAM

Shomali was born just outside Tehran, and her desserts are often perfumed with Iranian spices. You may at first wonder at her partnership with Suzanne Goin, whose preference is for seasonal Californian ingredients and the flavors of France and Italy. But what Shomali and Goin have in common is a confident hand. Their food is nuanced and layered but also unabashedly assertive. Here, the cardamom is front and center, set against a smooth, rich ice cream. This beauty of a recipe deserves very fresh green cardamom pods, not the ones that have been sitting on your shelf all year. Splurge, as those five little pods are the star of this dessert.

5 green cardamom pods

1⅓ cups heavy cream

1 cup whole milk

½ cup sugar

3 tablespoons light corn syrup

2 egg yolks

pinch of salt

¼ teaspoon freshly ground cardamom

½ teaspoon freshly squeezed lemon juice

Makes 1 quart

Crack open the cardamom pods by gently pressing each one with the back of a spoon. Don't let the precious seeds fall out!

Combine the cardamom pods with their seeds, the heavy cream, milk, sugar, and corn syrup in a saucepan and cook over medium heat, whisking frequently. As soon as you see the first stirrings of a simmer, remove from the heat. Leave the saucepan on the stove and let the cardamom infuse the dairy for half an hour.

Meanwhile, in a bowl, lightly whisk the egg yolks to break them up rather than froth them. Whisk in a pinch of salt.

Return the cardamom milk mixture almost to a simmer over medium heat, then slowly pour about a third of it into the yolks, while whisking constantly. Then pour the combined mixture back into the saucepan and continue to whisk. Return the mixture to a simmer and continue to cook for about 4 minutes, until it has thickened enough to coat the back of a spoon.

Prepare an ice bath. Strain the custard through a fine-mesh sieve into a metal bowl set in the ice bath and whisk occasionally until thoroughly chilled. Whisk in the ground cardamom and lemon juice.

Churn in an ice cream machine according to the manufacturer's instructions. Freeze in airtight containers for at least 2 hours before serving.

WHAT YOU NEED TO KNOW

Chocolate and cardamom like to dance together. So if you must sauce, go chocolate and go dark. Ground cardamom is best freshly ground. Simply grind the seeds in a coffee or spice grinder right before use.

Jessica Mortarotti and Zachary Cox of Carmela Ice Cream, Pasadena

SPICED APPLE SORBET

Please make this. Yes, that is a plea. It is one of the best sorbets I've ever had. I realize the name isn't sexy, so I wanted to tell you. The spices give a warm depth not often found in sorbet, and the generous dose of citrus keeps it bright and refreshing. It makes a perfect autumn dessert, paired perhaps with the Cranberry Thyme Sorbet (page 179), but it is also an ideal interlude or palate cleanser between a heavy main course and dessert. Thanksgiving naturally comes to mind.

3 apples, preferably Granny Smith

2 cups water

1¾ cups sugar

1 teaspoon allspice berries

½ teaspoon ground cinnamon

¼ teaspoon ground nutmeg

½ teaspoon whole cloves

2 teaspoons grated orange zest

1 tablespoon grated lemon zest

¼ teaspoon salt

2 tablespoons freshly squeezed lemon juice

Makes about 1 quart

Peel the apples, reserving their peel. Discard the core. Cut the flesh into rough cubes.

In a large pot, combine the water, sugar, apple peels, allspice, cinnamon, nutmeg, clove, zests, and salt and set over medium heat. Bring to a boil, whisking periodically. Lower the heat and simmer for 6 minutes.

While the spices are simmering, prepare an ice bath. Once the apple-spice mixture has simmered for 6 minutes, pour it straightaway into a metal bowl and set this bowl in the ice bath. Chill, whisking periodically, until cold. Add more ice to the ice bath, if needed.

Once cold, strain the mixture through a fine-mesh sieve, discarding the solids and reserving the syrup. Transfer the syrup to an airtight container. Refrigerate for up to 2 days. Give it a shake before using.

In a blender, combine the apple syrup, cubed apple, and lemon juice and puree until perfectly smooth. Strain through a fine-mesh sieve, discarding any stray seeds and pressing out all of the juice. Churn in an ice cream machine according to the manufacturer's instructions and freeze in airtight containers for at least 2 hours before serving.

WHAT YOU NEED TO KNOW

This is the moment for good Granny Smith apples. They have just the right sweet pucker for this recipe.

THE THREE ESSENTIAL ICE CREAM SAUCES

Lindsay Kirk and Brooke Williamson of Small Batch, Mar Vista

HOT TOFFEE SAUCE

Think hot liquid candy bar.

2 cups butter

2 packed cups light brown sugar

2 tablespoons bourbon

⅓ cup whole milk

¼ cup heavy cream

3 tablespoons light corn syrup

Nakes roughly 4 cups

Combine all of the ingredients in a pot over medium heat. Swirl the pot or stir to mix, taking care not to be splattered by the hot liquid. As soon as it boils, give it one last swirl and remove it from heat.

Prepare an ice bath. Pour the sauce into a metal bowl set in the ice bath. Let cool, stirring occasionally, then store in a covered jar in the refrigerator for up to 2 weeks. Serve hot.

Jeni Britton Bauer of Jeni's Splendid Ice Creams, Los Feliz

MAGIC HOT FUDGE

"This hot fudge is like magic," Britton Bauer told me. You take dry ingredients and melt them together, and they become a shiny, amazing warm sauce for ice cream.

¼ cup Dutch-processed cocoa

¼ cup sugar

¼ cup finely chopped bittersweet chocolate (preferably 70% cacao)

¼ cup boiling water

Makes roughly 1 cup

Combine the cocoa, sugar, and chocolate in a heat-proof bowl, then pour in the boiling water. Let stand for 2 minutes, then stir until thoroughly combined. Serve immediately.

Meadow Ramsey of Kismet, Los Feliz

VEGAN, DAIRY-FREE DATE CARAMEL

So healthy you could pour it over yogurt for breakfast.

8 ounces Medjool dates

¾ cup simmering water

½ cup freshly squeezed orange juice

4 tablespoons olive oil

¼ teaspoon salt

_____

Makes roughly 2 cups

Place the dates in a heatproof bowl and pour the simmering water over them. Set aside to soak for 7 minutes. Strain the dates and reserve the soaking water. If the dates need to be pitted, this should now be easy. If any skin is peeling away, remove entirely and discard.

Combine the pitted dates, reserved water, and orange juice in a blender and puree until smooth. Slowly drizzle in the olive oil while the blender continues to run. Add the salt and blend to incorporate. Strain through a fine-mesh sieve. Store in a covered jar and refrigerate for up to 2 days. Heat before serving.

SWEETS

Na Young Ma of Proof Bakery, Atwater Village

ORANGE CARDAMOM SHORTBREAD

When I called Ma to ask her to contribute a cookie recipe to this book, her first response was "yes!" but her second was "not the chocolate chip!" Of course, I thought, a serious pastry chef such as Ma wants to be known for more complicated fare. But she explained that the all-American staple is the hardest cookie for a baker and requires hands-on training, if the quality is to be consistent. I laughed when she then suggested this exquisite shortbread. It was already a favorite of mine, but I imagined that any recipe that so perfectly married a delicate crumb with a lasting structure to be quite challenging. Not so. Here, a small amount of whole wheat flour holds the cookie together in one piece.

1 cup butter, at room temperature

zest of 1 or 2 oranges

¾ cup confectioners' sugar

1⅔ cups all-purpose flour

½ cup whole wheat flour

1½ teaspoons freshly ground green cardamom seeds

½ teaspoon salt

Makes 15 cookies

Preheat the oven to 325°F.

In a large bowl, beat the butter and orange zest together with an electric mixer on low speed, or using the paddle attachment in a stand mixer, until the zest is dispersed in the butter.

Sift the confectioners' sugar into the bowl and beat until smooth and well incorporated, about 2 minutes.

Sift the flours, cardamom, and salt together onto a sheet of parchment or into a bowl, then fold them into the butter mixture.

Roll out the dough between two large sheets of parchment paper until it is ¼ inch thick. Either chill it in the fridge for 30 minutes or in the freezer for 15 minutes.

Line two cookie sheets with parchment paper.

Slice the dough in squares or rectangles about 2½ inches wide. Bake the cookies for 13 to 16 minutes, rotating the pans halfway through the baking time. The cookies should be just barely gold at the edges.

Cool on a wire rack. Store in an airtight container and eat within 2 days or freeze for up to 1 month.

WHAT YOU NEED TO KNOW

Orange and cardamom are a classic combination and one I happen to love. Freshly ground green cardamom is key. Simply remove the seeds from their pod and grind them in a coffee grinder or spice grinder until you have a fine powder. If you can, use French butter in this recipe for its slightly higher fat content.

Valerie Gordon of Valerie Confections, Silver Lake and Echo Park

ALMOND MATCHA SANDWICH COOKIE

Valerie has the precision of a master baker and the generous spirit of a cookie lover. She first became known for her exceptional chocolates, caramels, and toffees, but it wasn't long before her fanciful cookies and cakes took on cult status. These sandwich cookies are a favorite of mine and will please even a matcha skeptic. The sweetness of the white chocolate is offset by the depth of flavor in the toasted almond flour and in the two varieties of tea.

⅓ cup genmaicha or toasted rice tea

3½ cups almond flour

½ teaspoon kosher salt

14 tablespoons butter, at room temperature

½ cup granulated sugar

⅓ packed cup light brown sugar

2 teaspoons vanilla paste or vanilla extract

1⅔ cups white chocolate chips (preferably Valrhona)

2 tablespoons plus 1 teaspoon culinary-grade matcha powder

Makes about 36 cookies

Preheat the oven to 325°F.

Grind the genmaicha or toasted rice tea to a powder in a coffee grinder or Vitamix.

Toast about half of the almond flour until golden and fragrant on a rimmed baking sheet. Let cool completely before combining it with the remaining almond flour, the ground tea, and salt. Leave the oven on.

In the bowl of a stand mixer fitted with the paddle attachment, cream the butter and sugars on medium speed until light and fluffy, about 4 minutes.

With the mixer on low, add the dry ingredients in three additions, mixing well after each addition and scraping down the sides of the bowl each time. Add the vanilla paste and mix thoroughly.

Roll out half of the dough between two large sheets of parchment paper until it's about ⅛ inch thick. Slide the dough, still between the parchment sheets, onto a baking sheet or other flat surface and freeze until firm, about 15 minutes. Repeat with the remaining dough.

Using a 1½-inch round cookie cutter, cut the dough into rounds and place 1 to 2 inches apart on a parchment-lined baking sheet.

Bake the cookies for 10 to 12 minutes, rotating the sheets halfway through baking, until the edges are golden. Let the cookies cool on a wire rack.

Once the cookies are cool, pour the chocolate chips into a glass or ceramic heatproof bowl. Microwave for 15-second intervals, stirring after each interval, until just melted. Or melt the chocolate in a double boiler.

Sift the matcha onto the melted chocolate in two additions, stirring aggressively after each addition until incorporated and completely smooth. If the matcha chocolate is extremely fluid, wait for 5 to 8 minutes before using.

Place half of the cookies on a tray, flat side facing up, and spread about 1 teaspoon of matcha chocolate onto each cookie.

Gently press the remaining cookies on top of the matcha chocolate, so that the flat sides face each other. Let sit a few minutes before serving so the chocolate can set. These are best eaten the day they are made.

MACAROONS

When Britton Bauer started making these cookies, they were still referred to in America as macaroons with an "oo." She decided to let it stick. These cookies make a mean ice cream sandwich.

8 ounces nuts (1½ cups blanched whole almonds or 1 cup plus 2 tablespoons pistachios or 1½ cups toasted blanched whole hazelnuts)

2½ cups confectioners' sugar

¾ cup egg whites (from 6 or 7 large eggs), at room temperature

¼ teaspoon salt

½ cup plus 2 tablespoons granulated sugar

Makes 12 cookies

Line a large baking sheet with parchment paper. Using a 3-inch biscuit or cookie cutter as a guide, trace 12 circles on the parchment. This will ensure that the macaroons are the same size and will match up if and when paired to make an ice cream sandwich. Turn the sheet of parchment paper over.

Grind the nuts with ¼ cup of the confectioners' sugar in a food processor until a fine nut flour forms. Do not let the mixture become a paste. Add the remaining 2¼ cups of confectioners' sugar and pulse just until incorporated. If necessary, sift the mixture through a fine-mesh sieve and discard any large pieces of nuts.

Using the whisk attachment, whip the egg whites and salt in the bowl of a stand mixer until frothy. (Or use a handheld electric mixer and a large bowl.) Start on low speed and increase as the whites take shape. While the mixer is running, slowly add the granulated sugar, a spoonful at a time, and whip until the meringue is shiny and holds medium peaks, about 5 minutes.

Using a rubber spatula, fold in the nut flour, a third at a time, until thoroughly combined.

Fit a pastry bag with a ¼-inch plain tip and fill the bag halfway with the batter. Holding the bag upright, pipe macaroons inside the traced circles. Begin in the center of each circle and work your way out in a spiral.

Let the cookies sit at room temperature for 30 minutes to dry. This will create a crisp crust on the outside of the macaroon.

Preheat the oven to 300°F.

Bake the cookies for 18 to 20 minutes, rotating the sheet halfway through baking, until they have risen slightly and look crisp and set on top. Remove from the oven and let cool completely.

Slide the parchment sheet of macaroons onto another baking sheet and freeze; once they are frozen, transfer to a freezer bag or storage container. Be careful: macaroons are delicate. They can be frozen for up to 1 month.

WHAT YOU NEED TO KNOW

The choice of nuts is yours to make. When grinding nuts to make nut flour in a food processor, it helps to work with cold nuts and a cold blade. Refrigerate both if you have time. If you don't have a pastry bag, use a plastic freezer bag. Fill the bag, press out excess air, and seal, then cut about ¼ inch off one of the corners to create a "tip" from which to pipe.

TO MAKE ICE CREAM SANDWICHES

Place a frozen macaroon upside down on a work surface. Place a small scoop of ice cream on the cookie. You may also add a spoonful of room-temperature fudge or caramel sauce. Top with another cookie and gently press the cookies together until the ice cream comes to the edges of the macaroons. Wrap in wax paper, parchment paper, or plastic wrap and freeze. Sealed in an airtight container, the sandwiches will keep for up to 2 weeks.

BROWN BUTTER JAM BLONDIES

We all need a few back-pocket recipes that are easy, quick, and thoroughly satisfying. And this blondie is just that. Koslow has two tricks that take this classic to a new height. First, she browns the butter until it is truly brown. This is no time to wimp out. Second, she swirls jam through the batter before baking. Not enough to give the blondie a jammy taste or feel, but just enough so that, every few bites, the fruit squares off with the flakes of Maldon sea salt.

1½ cups butter

2⅔ packed cups dark brown sugar

1½ teaspoons fine sea salt

3 eggs, lightly whisked to break apart

1½ teaspoons vanilla extract

3 cups all-purpose flour

1½ teaspoons baking powder

¼ cup jam (such as raspberry, blackberry, or black currant)

maldon sea salt, for sprinkling

Makes 12 blondies

Preheat the oven to 350°F. Line the bottom and sides of a 9 by 13-inch baking pan with parchment paper.

Brown the butter in a skillet over medium heat until it darkens to a deep golden-brown. While it is still warm, stir in the brown sugar and sea salt. Whisk in the eggs and the vanilla. The mixture should be thick and glossy. Gently fold in the flour and baking powder and mix only until just incorporated.

Pour the batter into the prepared pan. Top with the jam and, using a knife, lightly swirl it into the surface of the batter. You don't need to go deep here. Sprinkle with a light shower of Maldon sea salt.

Bake for 25 to 30 minutes, or until a knife inserted in the center comes out clean of batter—it may, however, show signs of jam. Let cool in the pan for a few minutes, then transfer to a cooling rack. Cut into squares. The blondies may also be frozen, wrapped in plastic wrap, for up to 1 month.

WHAT YOU NEED TO KNOW

You may halve this recipe and bake it in an 8-inch square pan. Choose a jam that isn't too sweet. Strawberry is too soft a match, whereas black currant offers a stronger counterpoint to the richness of the blondie. Experiment too with spiced or spiked jam. Bourbon, ginger—strong accents will work best in this. Just don't be tempted to overdo the jam, as it will interrupt the blondie's texture.

FLEUR DE SEL BROWNIES

Lesser is known for making the best brittle in Los Angeles, which he sells from his website. But I am first and foremost a chocolate lover, and this brownie of his satisfies at both the primal and the culinary level. Dense, dark, moist, rich. Chocolate and cocoa, both. Very little flour to disrupt the immediate rush of endorphins. And a touch of fleur de sel or Maldon sea salt to fire up the palate. He also makes a spicy, chile-infused version, which I include here as well. Wonderful late at night with a glass of good tequila or mezcal.

10 ounces bittersweet chocolate (preferably Valrhona 70% cacao), broken up into pieces

¾ cup butter (preferably Plugrá or another European style)

1½ cups sugar

½ cup cocoa powder (preferably Valrhona)

1 teaspoon instant espresso powder

1 tablespoon vanilla extract

4 eggs

¾ cup plus 2 tablespoons all-purpose flour

1 teaspoon fleur de sel or 1½ teaspoons Maldon sea salt

Makes 12 brownies

Preheat the oven to 350°F. Line the bottom and sides of a 9 by 13-inch baking pan with parchment paper or aluminum foil.

Melt the chocolate and butter in a double boiler, stirring occasionally to marry the two together.

Combine the sugar, cocoa powder, and espresso powder in a large bowl or the bowl of a stand mixer. When the chocolate has melted, remove it from the heat and add it to the sugar mixture. Using either the paddle attachment of a stand mixer or a handheld electric mixer, quickly pulse on and off to meld the ingredients together.

Add the vanilla and then the eggs, one at a time, and mix until thoroughly incorporated. Add the flour and fleur de sel and quickly pulse on and off until the flour is well incorporated.

Pour the batter into the prepared pan and spread as evenly as possible. Bake for 18 to 22 minutes, rotating halfway through baking and popping any air bubbles with a toothpick, until the top looks just dry. Let the brownies cool to room temperature in the pan on a wire rack, then cut into 3-inch squares. Alternatively, place the pan in the fridge until well chilled and cut the brownies into shapes with a cookie cutter. Let come to room temperature before serving.

FOR SPICY BROWNIES

Add ½ teaspoon Saigon ground cinnamon, 1 teaspoon finely ground morita or dried chipotle chiles, and 1½ teaspoons Urfa Biber chile flakes to the sugar mixture.

Amanda Chantal Bacon of Moon Juice, Venice Beach

CARROT COCONUT VEGAN "PANNA COTTA"

Chantal Bacon was a chef before she started her juicing empire. In this recipe, her culinary talent is on full display. The sweetness of the carrots, the mellowness of the coconut, and the fiery heat of the ginger are expertly balanced. Bacon calls it a panna cotta, but the recipe is a vegan one and contains coconut milk instead of cream, and agar-agar instead of gelatin. It's a dessert but healthy enough for an afternoon snack.

½ cup plus 2 tablespoons freshly pressed and strained carrot juice

1 tablespoon agar-agar powder

1¼ cups full-fat coconut milk

¼ cup coconut sugar

½ teaspoon pink Himalayan sea salt

¾ teaspoon vanilla extract

½ teaspoon ground ginger

TOPPING

¼ cup chopped raw pistachios

¼ cup raw honey

1 teaspoon grated fresh ginger

½ cup minced crystallized ginger

Serves 3

Pour the carrot juice into a small bowl. Sprinkle with the agar-agar and give it a quick stir. Let the mixture sit undisturbed for 10 minutes so that the agar-agar can bloom, thickening the juice.

Meanwhile, combine ¼ cup of the coconut milk and the coconut sugar in a saucepan and cook over medium heat, whisking to combine. Continue cooking and whisking for 4 to 5 minutes, or until the sugar has dissolved and the mixture has thickened slightly. Then, continuing to whisk, add the remaining 1 cup coconut milk and the pink salt and bring to a simmer.

Turn the heat to low, add the carrot-agar mixture, and whisk to combine. Continue to cook until the mixture is just short of a simmer. Remove from the heat. Stir in the extract and the ground ginger.

Pour the mixture into 3 (5-ounce) ramekins or teacups and refrigerate, uncovered, for 1 hour. Cover with plastic wrap and refrigerate for at least 3 more hours and up to 24 hours.

Top as you'd like, with pistachios, honey, fresh ginger, and crystalized ginger, and serve.

WHAT YOU NEED TO KNOW

The topping is a key component to the recipe, as it offers texture and heightens the flavor. Play around with any combination of grated fresh ginger, minced candied ginger, chopped pistachios, and honey until you hit your sweet spot.

Zoe Nathan, Laurel Almerinda, and Bryant Ng of Cassia, Santa Monica

KAFFIR LIME PUDDING

Despite knowing that the avocado is a fruit, I've always found it hard to imagine it in a dessert with anything less than wariness and skepticism. Chef Ng wisely placed this beautiful pudding before me with no mention of its ingredients. I was immediately struck by the smooth, creamy texture, the bright burst of lime, the exotic undercurrent of kaffir lime leaves, the freshness of mint, and the heady rush of rum. It was only when I saw the recipe that I noticed the avocado in there. By then, I was already hooked. This one's a real beauty.

8 kaffir lime leaves

½ packed cup fresh mint leaves

½ cup sugar

½ cup freshly squeezed lime juice

zest of 2 limes, plus more for garnish

2 tablespoons crème fraîche

½ ripe large avocado

2 tablespoons white rum or cachaça

2½ cups heavy cream

Serves 5

Toss the kaffir lime leaves, mint, and sugar in a saucepan. Muddle the leaves into the sugar and set aside for 10 minutes.

Meanwhile, whizz the lime juice, lime zest, crème fraîche, and avocado until smooth in a blender. Add the rum and blend to combine. Transfer to a mixing bowl and set aside.

Add the cream to the sugar mixture and slowly bring the mixture to a boil, whisking occasionally to dissolve the sugar. Immediately remove from the heat and set aside, whisking occasionally, until the cream cools to room temperature.

Pour the cream mixture through a fine-mesh sieve into the juice mixture. Discard the muddled leaves. Whisk the custard and divide evenly among 5 ramekins.

Chill the ramekins in the fridge. After 1 hour, cover the puddings with plastic wrap. Chill for another 3 hours; it will take the puddings a total of 4 hours to set. They may be chilled overnight and served the following day. Top with a grating of lime zest.

WHAT YOU NEED TO KNOW

This is a softly set custard with a delicate consistency, similar to a British posset. Serve it in individual ramekins, teacups, glasses, little canning jars, or small bowls. At the restaurant, it's served with sliced strawberries or cherries tossed with a little lime zest. In a pinch, I've even made this without the kaffir lime leaves, which can be hard to find. Without them, the lime, mint, and rum simply take center stage. Different, but equally good.

FENNEL PAVLOVA WITH A STRAWBERRY FOOL

A classic with a twist. Fennel pollen lends a mysterious background note, rekindling an old romance.

PAVLOVA

6 egg whites

1½ cups sugar

2 teaspoons cornstarch

1 teaspoon distilled white vinegar

1 teaspoon fennel pollen

1 tablespoon freshly squeezed lemon juice

1 fresh shiso or mint leaf, cut into chiffonade

1½ teaspoons sugar

zest of ½ lemon

salt

STRAWBERRY FOOL

2 cups trimmed and halved peak-season fresh strawberries

TO SERVE

1 cup heavy cream

¼ cup toasted walnuts (optional)

Serves 6

WHAT YOU NEED TO KNOW

The addition of fennel pollen and a shiso leaf gives this pavlova an unexpected dimension, but neither are compulsory. Mint or spearmint may be used in place of the shiso. Centeno uses a piping bag to create individual meringues, but I use an offset spatula to make one large one knowing no one will pause to criticize the misshapen appearance of anything so tempting.

To make the pavlova, preheat the oven to 225°F. Line a large baking sheet with parchment paper.

Whip the egg whites in the bowl of a stand mixer fitted with the whisk attachment or with a handheld electric mixer on high speed until they hold firm peaks.

Gently fold in the sugar until combined, followed by the cornstarch, vinegar, and fennel pollen.

Transfer the meringue into a piping bag and pipe a large circle, square, or rectangle of the meringue directly onto the parchment paper. It's easiest to start in the middle and work your way out. The edge should be slightly higher than the center.

Bake the pavlova until it easily pulls away from the parchment, about 1 hour. Transfer the parchment paper with the pavlova to a wire rack to cool. The pavlova may be made up to 3 hours in advance and kept at room temperature somewhere dry.

To make the strawberry fool, in a large bowl, gently mix the strawberries, lemon juice, shiso, sugar, lemon zest, and a pinch of salt. Set aside to macerate for 15 minutes.

After 15 minutes, remove 1 cup of the macerated strawberries and transfer to a saucepan. Add a pinch of salt. Cook the strawberries over medium-low heat until they break down and become jammy, 10 to 12 minutes. Remove from the heat, transfer to another bowl, and set aside in the refrigerator to chill.

To serve, whip the heavy cream with a whisk or using a handheld electric mixer until soft peaks form. Gently fold in the cooked strawberries, just to swirl them through the whipped cream.

Spoon the whipped cream into the center of the pavlova. Top with the remaining macerated strawberries and sprinkle with the toasted walnuts. Serve immediately.

SQIRL

Jessica Koslow hit the right spot at the right time. Just as Silver Lake was becoming chic and a hunger for decadent-healthy food was growing, Koslow opened up her sidewalk café on a desolate strip that, thanks to her, is now a destination, most recognizable for the long line that seemingly exists in perpetuity outside Sqirl. Those patient folks are waiting for their daily dose of Koslow's justly famed thick slices of burnt brioche bread slathered with fresh ricotta and homemade jam. Or perhaps for their fix of bracing turmeric tonics. Lunchtime, however, is definitely for bowls of Sorrel Pesto Rice and perhaps a Lait 'N'Egg coffee and a Brown Butter Jam Blondie (page 203) for dessert.

TOASTED SESAME CAKE

This is unlike any cake I've ever had, and it sparked love at first bite. Chef Hopson told me he wanted to create a dessert that was familiar—a cake with nuts—but with sesame as the star. The cake is terrific entirely unadorned and eaten as a snack straight from the pan or served with a dollop of crème fraîche at supper. But for a party, try it with a brushing of orange syrup.

CAKE

1⅓ cups sugar

⅓ cup plus ¾ cup all-purpose flour

1 cup sesame paste (see recipe)

1 cup cold butter, cut into cubes

1 tablespoon vanilla paste

1 tablespoon sesame oil

6 eggs

2 teaspoons baking powder

1 teaspoon salt

orange syrup (see recipe)

crème fraîche

———

Serves 6

Preheat the oven to 325°F. Butter a 9-inch square baking pan.

Combine the sugar, ⅓ cup of the flour, and the sesame paste in a food processor and pulse until smooth. Add the cold butter, vanilla paste, and sesame oil and pulse until smooth. Add the eggs, one at a time, and pulse until smooth, scraping the sides of the bowl once or twice. Finally, add the baking powder, salt, and the remaining ¾ cup of the flour and pulse until smooth.

Pour the cake batter into the prepared pan and bake for 35 to 45 minutes, or until the center is set and a cake tester comes out clean.

If you are using the orange syrup, warm it up. While the cake is still warm and in the pan, prick it two dozen times with the tip of a short knife. Drizzle or brush with as much of the syrup as you wish.

Serve the cake cut into squares at room temperature or still slightly warm with a dollop of crème fraîche.

WHAT YOU NEED TO KNOW

Don't be tempted to use store-bought sesame paste here. The results won't be as fabulous.

Sesame Paste Makes 1 cup

1 cup sesame seeds

¼ cup sugar

2 tablespoons water

1 tablespoon honey

Toast the sesame seeds in a dry skillet over low heat until they are a golden brown and aromatic. Transfer to a plate and set aside to cool to room temperature. In a food processor, combine the toasted sesame seeds, sugar, water, and honey and process until smooth. This may be made up to a week in advance and stored in the refrigerator, then brought to room temperature before using.

Orange Syrup

½ cup sugar

½ cup freshly squeezed orange juice

½ cup water

zest of 1 orange

1 teaspoon orange blossom water, or to taste

Combine the sugar, juice, water, and zest in a small saucepan and bring to a boil. Remove from the heat and set aside somewhere warm until ready to use. Add the orange blossom water.

Sahar Shomali of Lucques, Melrose

BOURBON CHERRY CRISP

Shomali makes a mean bourbon chocolate-chip cookie and a rich chocolate bourbon cake, but her bourbon cherry crisp is positively adults-only. It's not lightly scented with a mere whiff of whiskey, but full-out boozy and bold. Taking a bite is a bit like taking a swig, eating a ripe cherry, and munching on a crunchy cookie, all at the same time. The three elements remain defiantly distinct, while also coming together in the guise of that warm, familiar, and comforting American classic: the fruit crisp.

This crisp is rustic enough to serve outside in tin bowls after a meal cooked on the grill, and it is equally suited to an elegant dinner party. As the bourbon flavor is pronounced, choose one that you like to drink. A crowning scoop of vanilla ice cream will temper the alcohol's heat.

BOURBON CHERRIES

⅔ cup unsweetened dried cherries

⅔ cup bourbon

CRUMBLE TOPPING

1¾ cups all-purpose flour

½ cup granulated sugar

⅔ packed cup dark brown sugar

½ teaspoon salt

¼ teaspoon ground cinnamon

¼ teaspoon freshly grated nutmeg

12 tablespoons cold butter, cut into cubes

CRISP

6 cups pitted fresh cherries

3 tablespoons granulated sugar

3 tablespoons freshly squeezed orange juice

⅛ teaspoon salt

vanilla ice cream, for serving

Serves 6

To make the bourbon cherries, in a small bowl, pour the bourbon over the dried cherries. Let sit at room temperature for at least 4 hours and up to 8 hours. Do not strain.

To make the crumble topping, mix together the flour, sugars, salt, cinnamon, and nutmeg in a bowl. Add the butter and use your fingers to massage it into the flour mixture until the consistency resembles a coarse meal. Refrigerate for half an hour before baking.

Meanwhile, preheat the oven to 350°F.

To make the crisp, in a large bowl, toss together the fresh cherries, the bourbon cherries, the sugar, orange juice, and salt. Pour this mixture into a 9-inch square baking pan or deep pie dish. Top with the crumble. Bake until the top is golden brown and the cherry filling is bubbling, 30 to 40 minutes.

Serve warm with a scoop of vanilla ice cream.

WHAT YOU NEED TO KNOW

Unless you want scary red fingers, invest in a cherry pitter. It makes this recipe quick and easy. Plan B is rubber gloves. The crisp topping freezes well, so make a double batch. You will want to make this again.

CHOCOLATE SESAME CAKE

Ramsey ingeniously uses toasted buckwheat flour to give this moist chocolate cake an earthy undertone. She then presses toasted sesame seeds onto the batter before baking the cake in a bain-marie. The sesame seeds draw upon the savory Middle Eastern dishes at Kismet while also adding crunch and protein. At the restaurant, it is served with the Buckwheat Ice Cream (page 182) and Vegan, Dairy-Free Date Caramel (page 193), but a simple dollop of crème fraîche is the ultimate shortcut to bliss.

¼ cup buckwheat or all-purpose flour

½ cup sesame seeds (optional)

12 ounces bittersweet chocolate (preferably Valrhona 70% cacao)

1 cup butter, cut into pieces

1 teaspoon vanilla extract

½ cup sugar

¼ teaspoon salt

¼ cup water

6 eggs

———

Serves 6

Preheat the oven to 300°F.

If using buckwheat flour, spread it on a rimmed baking sheet and bake for 1 hour, shaking the pan occasionally.

Spread the sesame seeds on a second rimmed baking sheet and also bake for 1 hour, shaking the pan occasionally to turn the seeds.

Transfer each to its own bowl and let cool for 15 minutes. Leave the oven on. Set a kettle of water to boil for the bain-marie.

Line a 9- or 10-inch round cake pan with enough parchment paper to create a 2-inch overhang. You will need the overhang to lift the cake out of the pan.

Melt the chocolate and the butter together in a double boiler. Stir in the vanilla extract.

In a small saucepan, combine the sugar and salt with the water. Bring to a simmer over medium heat, stirring constantly, until the sugar and salt have dissolved and the syrup has thickened. Whisk the syrup into the melted chocolate in a steady stream.

Whisk in the eggs, one at a time. Whisk in the flour, bit by bit.

Pour the batter into the prepared cake pan. If using, sprinkle the sesame seeds onto the batter so that they are evenly distributed over the cake's surface.

Fold a dish towel in quarters and place in a wide skillet or roasting pan. Place the cake pan on top of the dish towel. Fill the skillet or roasting pan with enough boiling water to reach halfway up the side of the cake pan to make a bain-marie. Taking care not to splash any water onto the batter, transfer the bain-marie to the oven.

Bake for 30 minutes, rotating the pan once. Remove from the oven. Let the cake sit for 10 minutes in the bain-marie, then transfer it to a wire rack. Let it come to room temperature, then transfer it, still in the cake pan, to the fridge. Chill for at least 4 hours and up to 24 hours. Remove it from the fridge 20 minutes before serving.

WHAT YOU NEED TO KNOW

This recipe is equally good with all-purpose flour. And the sesame seeds are entirely optional.

Zoe Nathan and Laurel Almerinda, Cassia, Santa Monica

VIETNAMESE COFFEE PUDDING

This pudding is catnip for coffee lovers. An intense hit of coffee enveloped in a rich creaminess makes this utterly irresistible.

¼ cup espresso beans

1 cup sweetened condensed milk

½ cup whole milk

½ cup heavy cream

1 vanilla bean, split lengthwise

½ cup brewed espresso

3 eggs

3 tablespoons sugar

2 tablespoons cornstarch

⅛ tsp kosher salt

3 tablespoons butter, cut into cubes, at room temperature

¾ teaspoon vanilla extract

whipped cream, for serving

Serves 4 to 6

Crush the espresso beans with the flat side of a knife or pulse them briefly in a coffee grinder to break them up, but not turn them into grounds.

In a medium saucepan, combine the condensed milk, whole milk, heavy cream, vanilla bean, crushed espresso beans, and espresso. Cook over low heat, whisking occasionally, until it just begins to simmer. Immediately remove from the heat and let steep for 30 minutes.

Whisk together the eggs, sugar, cornstarch, and salt in a mixing bowl.

Bring the cream mixture back to a simmer and, whisking constantly, slowly pour about a third into the eggs. Pour the combined mixture back into the saucepan and bring it back to a simmer. Do not stop whisking. Cook for about 4 minutes, or until it has thickened enough to coat the back of a spoon.

Strain the custard through a fine-mesh sieve into a clean bowl and whisk in the butter and vanilla.

Press a piece of plastic wrap to the surface of the custard to prevent a skin from forming and refrigerate for at least 4 hours until chilled through and set. Serve, chilled, with a dollop of whipped cream.

WHAT YOU NEED TO KNOW

This can also be served in individual cups, jars, or ramekins. It also makes one of the best coffee ice creams I've ever tasted. The steps are exactly the same until it comes time to cool down the custard. To make ice cream, place the custard in an ice bath and whisk it as it cools so that it does not set. Churn the cooled custard in an ice cream machine and freeze for 2 hours before serving.

PISTACHIO SEMOLINA CAKE

This rose, cardamom, and orange-scented pistachio cake is redolent with the flavors of the Middle East. Nut flours keep it moist, and semolina keeps it light.

CAKE

1⅓ cups butter, at room temperature

2 cups sugar

¾ teaspoon salt

4 eggs

1 tablespoon vanilla extract

1 tablespoon rose water

zest and juice of 1 orange

1⅓ cups semolina flour

2 cups ground pistachios plus ½ cup chopped pistachios

1½ cups almond flour

1¾ teaspoons baking powder

2 tablespoons sanding sugar

CARDAMOM ROSE WATER SYRUP

⅓ cup freshly squeezed tangerine, clementine, or orange juice

⅓ cup sugar

2 green cardamom pods, crushed

1 tablespoon rose water

Makes a 10-inch cake

WHAT YOU NEED TO KNOW

Rose waters vary in intensity, so add it to the syrup 1 teaspoon at a time, taste, and continue. For a stronger citrus taste, simply add 1 teaspoon of zest to the glaze. Nut flour gets stale so quickly that it is best to grind it yourself in a food processor. I find it helpful to chill the blade and add a few spoonfuls of the sugar to the processor. Use the pulse button, as you don't want to end up with nut butter. This cake may be made a day in advance and stored, covered, at room temperature.

Preheat the oven to 350°F. Butter a 10-inch cake pan and line the bottom with parchment paper.

To make the cake, cream the butter, sugar, and salt together until pale with a handheld electric mixer or in the bowl of a stand mixer. Add the eggs, one at a time, beating well after each addition. Add the vanilla, rose water, and orange zest and juice and beat to fully integrate.

Combine the semolina, ground pistachios, almond flour, and baking powder in a mixing bowl and whisk to thoroughly combine. Fold the wet ingredients into the dry ingredients, then pour the batter into the prepared cake pan.

Top the batter with the chopped pistachios and sprinkle with the sanding sugar. Set aside for 10 minutes before transferring to the oven and baking for 45 to 55 minutes, or until the tip of a knife inserted in the center of the cake comes out clean.

While the cake is baking, make the cardamom rose water syrup by combining the juice, sugar, and cardamom in a saucepan over low heat. Stir to the dissolve the sugar and cook until the liquid is reduced by half. Set aside to cool to room temperature, then stir in the rose water to combine. Strain through a fine-mesh sieve and discard the cardamom pods.

Remove the cake from the oven and immediately pour on half of the syrup. Wait 15 minutes for the cake to absorb it and then repeat again if serving immediately. If serving later in the day, wait to give the cake its final dose of syrup until just before serving. The cake may be served straight from the pan or inverted onto a serving plate.

COCKTAILS

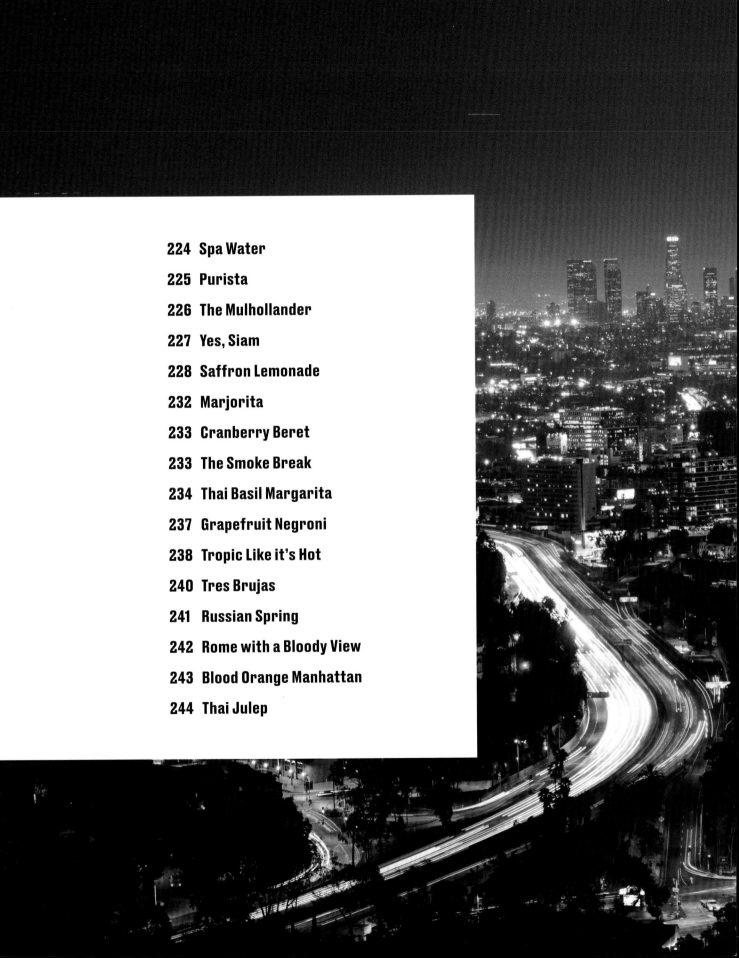

SPA WATER

Inspired by the cucumber-infused water served at spas. But, really, it's the vodka here that pampers weary bones and sore muscles.

3 slices Persian cucumber, plus a round slice, for garnish

3 ounces vodka (such as Purity)

½ ounce St. Germain elderflower liqueur

½ ounce freshly squeezed lime juice

Makes 1 cocktail

Muddle 3 of the cucumber slices in a shaker. Add the vodka, St. Germain, lime juice, and ice. Shake until well chilled and strain into a martini glass. Garnish with the remaining cucumber slice on the rim.

PURISTA

A Purista is similar to a margarita, but the triple sec has been replaced with a few dashes of orange bitters. The result is a cocktail that is less sweet and a favorite among tequila aficionados.

1 tablespoon coarse kosher salt

½ teaspoon sugar

slice of lime

2 ounces reposado tequila, (such as El Charro)

½ ounce agave nectar

1 ounce freshly squeezed lime juice

2 dashes of orange bitters (such as Fee Brothers West Indian Orange Bitters)

Makes 1 cocktail

Mix the salt and sugar on a small plate. Run the lime around the rim of your glass, then dip the rim into the salt and sugar mix. Set aside.

Combine the tequila, agave, lime juice, and bitters in a chilled, ice-filled cocktail shaker and shake gently but thoroughly to combine and chill. Strain into the rimmed glass and add a few cubes of fresh ice.

WHAT YOU NEED TO KNOW

Unless you are a professional mixologist or passionate amateur, there are really only three bitters to keep stocked: Angostura, Peychaud's, and orange. And when it comes to orange, there are two leading, widely available contenders to consider: Regan's Orange Bitters, which has a strong cardamom note, and Fee Brothers West Indian Orange Bitters, which is richly infused with orange zest. Try the Fee Brothers here, as it lends itself well to the purity of this simple Mexican cocktail.

THE MULHOLLANDER

It would be hard to find a duo as cool as Matt Alper and Walt Goggins. Alper shoots movies, Goggins stars in them. They like a good drink. They like working together. They finish each other's sentences. Their bromance led to Mulholland Distilling. That it has taken off, however, is not due only to their star power, but to the sheer drinkability of their booze. Their gin has hints of cucumber, lavender and lime. Their vodka has notes of mint. And sweet corn and maple take a little edge off their whiskey.

1½ ounces whiskey
(preferably Mulholland
American whiskey)

1½ ounces pineapple juice

1 ounce dry vermouth

¼ ounce freshly squeezed
lemon juice

1 fresh sage leaf

Makes 1 cocktail

Combine the whiskey, pineapple juice, vermouth, and lemon juice in an ice-filled cocktail shaker. Shake and strain into a chilled coupe glass. Garnish with the sage leaf.

Tobin Shea of Redbird, Downtown Arts District

YES, SIAM

Taking inspiration from the flavors of pad Thai, this cocktail transports you to the streets of Bangkok with a little help from a good Mexican mezcal, a Californian-Italian amaro, and a Venezuelan crème de cacao.

1½ ounces mezcal

½ ounce Amaro Angeleno

½ ounce crème de cacao (preferably Tempus Fugit)

¾ ounce freshly squeezed lime juice

¾ ounce tamarind syrup (see recipe)

TAMARIND SYRUP

1 cup water

1 cup sugar

1 ounce tamarind paste

Makes 1 cocktail

Combine all of the ingredients in an ice-filled shaker and shake until chilled. Strain into a chilled cocktail glass.

To make the Tamarind Syrup, combine the water, sugar, and tamarind paste in a small saucepan and bring to a boil over high heat. Lower the heat and simmer for 20 minutes, stirring occasionally to dissolve the sugar and paste. Set aside to bring to room temperature.

Many cocktails require special syrups or infusions. The rule of thumb is that syrups may be kept refrigerated in a sealed glass jar for up to a week and infused alcohol up to two weeks. Infused alcohols that do not contain any fresh ingredients, but are instead infused with spices, such as the saffron-infused tequila on page 229, may be stored in a cool, dark spot for up to one month.

SAFFRON LEMONADE

My idea of a perfect afternoon would be a few hours at the Broad Museum and then, as the sun sets, a glass or two of this spiked lemonade, sitting outdoors at nearby Otium. It's a burst of citrus with lingering notes of spice and a bit of heat, all softened with a honey simple syrup. And it's gorgeous to boot.

10 ounces saffron-infused tequila (see recipe)

5 ounces yellow Chartreuse

7½ ounces freshly squeezed lemon juice

7½ ounces freshly squeezed grapefruit

5 ounces honey simple syrup (see recipe)

20 dashes of orange bitters (preferably Regan's)

10 dashes of bird's eye chile tincture (see recipe)

chamomile buds, for garnish (optional)

Makes 4 cocktails or a small pitcher

Pour all of the ingredients into a large mason jar or sealable pitcher and give it a gentle but thorough shaking. Serve over ice. Float the buds.

WHAT YOU NEED TO KNOW

If you can't source fresh chamomile buds, simply use whole bud chamomile tea. There's no need to reconstitute them. The tincture needs 2 weeks to infuse, so plan ahead for this one.

Saffron-Infused Tequila

2 tablespoons boiling water

1 teaspoon saffron

10 ounces blanco tequila

Pour the boiling water over the saffron to bloom it. Set aside. When it comes to room temperature, combine it with the tequila. Alternatively, add the saffron directly to the tequila and let infuse for 24 hours.

Honey Simple Syrup

¾ cup honey

½ cup water

Bring the water and honey to a simmer in a small saucepan and stir to combine. Continue to cook for about 5 minutes to evaporate some of the water. Remove from the heat. Once at room temperature, transfer to the refrigerator until ready to use or for up to a week. Give it a shake before using.

Bird's Eye Chile Tincture

1 cup white rum

2 tablespoons bird's eye chile, chopped

Combine the rum and chile in a jar and refrigerate for 2 weeks. Give the jar a little shake every day. Strain through a fine-mesh sieve into a clean jar and refrigerate until ready to use.

OTIUM

One of the pleasures of going to a great museum, such as the Broad, is the afterglow—you leave the museum but continue to see art and beauty everywhere you look, as if your vision has expanded, as no doubt it has. It must be said that crossing the pavilion from the Broad to Otium heightens this experience. The restaurant's boxy steel and glass space juxtaposes the warm familiar smell of wood smoke with the plasticity of a Damien Hirst mural of a fish. But it's the truly open kitchen that seems to most connect to the airiness of the Broad and the vibrant public space its founder, Eli Broad, has created. That, and then there's that odd, entirely unscientific fact that good art makes people hungry for good food. It's all part and parcel of the same human need to live fully and urgently and never settle for the mundane.

Aaron Ranf of Rustic Canyon, Santa Monica

MARJORITA

Here, cucumber mellows a hit of habanero chiles, St. Germain offers a hint of floral and berry notes, and mint and lime give this tequila cocktail a bright freshness.

¾ ounce freshly squeezed lime juice

¼ ounce freshly pressed cucumber juice

¼ ounce simple syrup

5 fresh mint leaves, plus one more to float

2 ounces reposado tequila (such as Dos Armadillos)

½ ounce St. Germain elderflower liqueur

2 dashes of habanero tincture (see recipe)

1 thin slice jalapeño chile

Makes 1 cocktail

Place a large ice cube in a chilled glass.

Muddle the lime juice, cucumber juice, simple syrup, and 5 of the mint leaves. Add the tequila, St. Germain, and habanero tincture and shake with ice. Strain over the ice cube. Float the jalapeño slice and the mint leaf.

Habanero Tincture

10 habanero chiles, sliced

1¼ cups vodka

Soak the habanero slices in the vodka for 1 week in the refrigerator. Strain and use it like bitters to add heat to cocktails. Using a dropper might be the easiest way to control amounts.

Nate Reed of Rustic Canyon, Santa Monica

CRANBERRY BERET

This is pretty, light, and fizzy and makes the perfect aperitif to Thanksgiving dinner.

1 ounce vodka (such as Loft and Bear)

½ ounce orange liqueur (such as Leopold Bros.)

½ ounce cranberry liqueur (such as Leopold Bros.)

⅓ ounce freshly squeezed lime juice

¼ ounce simple syrup

2 ounces dry Prosecco

1 lemon twist, for garnish

Measure the vodka, the liqueurs, the lime juice, and simple syrup into an ice-filled cocktail shaker and give it a good 20 shakes. Strain into a flute. Top with Prosecco. Garnish with the lemon twist.

Makes 1 cocktail

Ori Menashe of Bestia, Downtown Arts District

THE SMOKE BREAK

Smoky mezcal wakes to a burst of lime and bittersweet notes from Cappelletti.

1½ ounces mezcal

¾ ounce Cappelletti or Campari (see note)

¾ ounce freshly squeezed lime juice

½ ounce orgeat

2 dashes of Angostura bitters

Shake all of the ingredients vigorously in an ice-filled cocktail shaker, then strain into a chilled coupe glass.

WHAT YOU NEED TO KNOW

Cappelletti is a red aperitivo. Almost a marriage of Campari and sweet vermouth, it has notes of sweet orange and bitter herbs. If using Campari, you might want to add ¼ ounce of simple syrup or mix equal parts Campari and sweet vermouth.

Makes 1 cocktail

Kenny Arbuckle of Cassia, Santa Monica

THAI BASIL MARGARITA

In this riff on a classic margarita, Thai basil offers a sweet herbaceous note.

salt, for rimming the glass (optional)

1 slice of lime or kaffir lime

2 ounces blanco tequila

¾ ounce Thai basil syrup (see recipe)

¾ ounce freshly squeezed lime juice

Makes 1 cocktail

Place the salt on a small plate. Run the lime over the rim of a glass, then dip the rim into the salt. Set aside.

Combine the remaining ingredients in an ice-filled cocktail shaker and shake for 20 seconds. Fill the rimmed glass with ice and strain the cocktail into it.

Thai Basil Syrup

1 cup fresh Thai basil leaves

1 cup simple syrup

Place the leaves in a blender with the simple syrup, blend, and strain through a fine-mesh sieve. Refrigerate until ready to use or for up to a week.

GRAPEFRUIT NEGRONI

Gin is a fantastic catalyst for citrus, and grapefruit lends itself particularly well to its bright botanicals.

1 ounce grapefruit-infused gin (see recipe)

1 ounce Campari

1 ounce Carpano Antica sweet vermouth

1 orange twist, for garnish

GRAPEFRUIT-INFUSED GIN

1 ounce grapefruit zest

12 ounces gin (such as London dry)

Makes 1 cocktail

Pour the gin, Campari, and vermouth over ice and stir or shake in a chilled cocktail shaker and strain into a glass. Float the orange twist.

To infuse the gin, combine the zest and gin in a glass mason jar. The jar does not need to be sealed shut, but it should be tightly closed. Set aside and let infuse somewhere out of direct sunlight for 2 or 3 days. Strain and use as needed. Refrigerate for up to 1 month.

WHAT YOU NEED TO KNOW

It's important that the glass container you use to infuse the gin be entirely clean of odor, as the gin will pick up any lingering scents. When zesting the grapefruit, avoid catching any of the pith, as it is quite bitter. The infusion takes a few days, so plan ahead.

Helen Johannesen of Son of a Gun, Beverly Grove

TROPIC LIKE IT'S HOT

This one all but screams beach party.

2 ounces blanco tequila

1½ ounces pineapple juice
(preferably freshly juiced
and strained)

¾ ounce freshly squeezed
lemon juice

¾ ounce simple syrup

2 dashes of orange bitters

1 dash of Angostura bitters
(optional)

pineapple slice, for garnish

Combine the first six ingredients in a chilled cocktail shaker. Shake and strain over fresh ice into a glass. Garnish with the pineapple slice.

Makes 1 cocktail

TRES BRUJAS

Ancho Reyes is made from steeping ancho chiles in a spirit made from sugarcane. Made in Puebla, Mexico, this liqueur has a sweet, smoked, spicy heat to it. Here, it offers complexity and fire. In a pinch, use passion fruit sorbet in place of the passion fruit simple syrup.

2 ounces Ancho Reyes

1 ounce freshly squeezed lime juice

1 ounce pineapple juice, freshly pressed and strained

3 ounces passion fruit simple syrup (see recipe) or passion fruit sorbet

1 lime slice, for garnish

Shake all of the ingredients in an ice-filled cocktail shaker. Strain into a chilled glass and garnish with the lime slice.

Makes 1 cocktail

Passion Fruit Simple Syrup

1 cup water

1 cup sugar

½ cup unsweetened passion fruit puree

Combine the water and sugar in a saucepan and bring to a boil. Lower the heat to a simmer and stir to dissolve the sugar. Continue to cook for 5 minutes to reduce the liquid to a syrup. Remove from the heat and let sit for 20 minutes to cool. Stir in the passion fruit puree and refrigerate in a sealed glass jar until ready to use.

RUSSIAN SPRING

This riff on a kir royale is just as lovely and quite a bit stronger, thanks to the vodka.

1 ounce vodka

¼ ounce crème de cassis

¾ ounce freshly squeezed lemon juice

¾ ounce raspberry simple syrup (see recipe)

3 ounces Champagne

Combine the first four ingredients in an ice-filled shaker and shake until chilled. Strain into a chilled flute and top with Champagne.

Makes 1 cocktail

Raspberry Simple Syrup

1 cup rich syrup (see recipe)

½ cup fresh or thawed frozen raspberries

Combine the syrup and berries in a blender and pulse until smooth. Strain through a fine-mesh sieve.

Rich Syrup

1 cup sugar

½ cup water

Combine the water and sugar in a saucepan and cook over low heat until all of the sugar has dissolved. Cool to room temperature. Rich Syrup may be stored in a glass jar in the fridge.

ROME WITH A BLOODY VIEW

Complex and intriguing, this cocktail will leave you guessing its origins.

1 ounce Leopold Bros. Aperitivo

1 ounce pineapple- and lemongrass-infused dry vermouth (see recipe)

1 ounce freshly squeezed lime juice

¾ ounce blood orange syrup (see recipe)

sparkling water

orange zest, for garnish

black pepper

Makes 1 cocktail

Combine the first four ingredients in an ice-filled shaker. Shake and strain into an ice-filled glass. Top with sparkling water, float the orange zest, and give it a quick grating of black pepper.

WHAT YOU NEED TO KNOW

The Leopold Bros. Aperitivo is something of a dry cousin to Campari and Aperol. A bit sweet, a bit bitter, quite dry, and brightly citrusy, it stands up to the depth of blood orange and the pine notes of dry vermouth.

Pineapple- and Lemongrass-Infused Dry Vermouth

1½ cups dry vermouth (such as Dolin)

½ cup chopped lemongrass

1 cup cubed ripe pineapple

Combine all of the ingredients in a mason jar. Seal and refrigerate for 24 hours to infuse. Strain through a fine-mesh sieve into a clean mason jar and keep refrigerated until needed.

Blood Orange Syrup

10 blood oranges (preferably organic), peeled and juiced

sugar, as needed

1 tablespoon black peppercorns

Measure the juice and combine with an equal amount of sugar, for a 1:1 ratio.

Combine the juice, orange peels, sugar, and peppercorns in a saucepot and bring to a simmer. Cook, stirring, for 10 minutes, to dissolve the sugar and thicken the liquid. Let come to room temperature. Strain into a clean jar and chill.

Ann-Marie Verdi of the Bellwether, Studio City

BLOOD ORANGE MANHATTAN

Not too sweet, not too sour, this is an intuitive twist on the classic Manhattan.

2 ounces blood orange bourbon (see recipe)

1 ounce Carpano Antica sweet vermouth

2 drops of blood orange bitters (such as Regan's)

1 blood orange twist

Makes 1 cocktail

Pour over ice and stir or shake in a chilled cocktail shaker and strain. Float the twist.

WHAT YOU NEED TO KNOW

It's important that the glass container you use to infuse the bourbon be entirely clean of odor, as the alcohol will pick up any lingering scents.

Blood Orange Bourbon

12 ounces blood oranges (preferably organic)

2 cups bourbon (such as Four Roses Yellow Label)

Wash the blood oranges and slice into rings. Toss the seeds. Combine the oranges, whatever juice has accumulated on the cutting board, and the bourbon in a mason jar and close. The jar does not need to be sealed shut, but it should be tightly closed. Set aside in the refrigerator to infuse for 5 days. Strain through a fine-mesh sieve and use as needed. It will keep refrigerated for up to 1 month.

THAI JULEP

This cocktail speaks to so much of what I love about Los Angeles food and drink. It tastes fresh, thanks to the lime, lemongrass, and pineapple. It's assertive thanks to the Thai chile tincture. It mixes Mexican tequila with Thai flavors and throws in a bit of Caribbean rum to keep you guessing. And then there's that kaffir lime leaf shrub in the background, giving it a contemporary-retro spin.

1 ounce rum

1 ounce blanco tequila

¾ ounce Thai shrub (see recipe)

¾ ounce freshly squeezed lime juice

½ ounce lemongrass coconut simple syrup (see recipe)

4 dashes of Thai chile tincture (see recipe)

pineapple wedge, for garnish

thai basil leaf, for garnish

Makes 1 cocktail

Combine all of the ingredients except for the garnishes in a shaker. Add a pinch of crushed ice and shake until the ice has dissolved. Pour into a double old-fashioned glass and top with crushed ice. Garnish with a pineapple wedge and float the Thai basil leaf.

WHAT YOU NEED TO KNOW

The Thai chile tincture takes 2 weeks to infuse.

Thai Shrub

1 cup pineapple chunks

½ cup fresh Thai basil leaves

3 kaffir lime leaves

1¼ cups sugar

1 cup vinegar (preferably coconut vinegar)

Combine all of the ingredients except the vinegar in a nonreactive bowl and stir to incorporate. Refrigerate for at least 1 day, 2 if possible. The sugar should be wet, but not liquidy. Add the vinegar and stir to dissolve. Strain through a fine-mesh sieve into a clean jar and refrigerate until ready to use.

Lemongrass Coconut Simple Syrup

2 stalks lemongrass, chopped

1¼ cups sugar

½ cup coconut water

Combine all of the ingredients in a saucepan and cook, stirring, over low heat to dissolve the sugar. Remove from the heat and set aside to steep for an hour. Strain with a fine-mesh sieve into a clean jar and refrigerate until ready to use.

Thai Chile Tincture

1 cup white rum (such as Wray and Nephew)

2 tablespoons chopped Thai chile

Combine the rum and chile in a jar and refrigerate for 2 weeks. Give it a little shake every day. Strain into a clean jar and refrigerate until ready to use.

ACKNOWLEDGMENTS

Not so long ago, I was in the back of a taxi with my twelve-year-old son, Garrick, when he turned to me and said, "If you need to spend the rest of the day on your book, you should. I want you to have the chance to do it right." If ever there was a more tender, more galvanizing offer, I've yet to hear it. What Garrick intuitively sensed was that I had hit that moment that happens to all writers in the writing of a book when said writer needs a second wind to fill the proverbial sails and drive the boat home. And that needed burst of energy doesn't come from looking at the calendar and seeing the looming deadline. That's called stress. Nor does it come necessarily from one's own inner reserves of strength. Those might have been depleted some time ago. It comes from those closest to you, and if you're lucky, it comes from a very sweet boy offering to give up weekend plans because he believes in you and what you are doing. Thank you, Garrick, for being wise and generous beyond your years. This book, my darling, is for you.

Most husband-and-wife writers would be the first to say that such commingled lives are both a blessing and a curse. There's never that "Honey, I'm home!" moment at the end of the day. Writers don't come home. They are home. And so it is all the more amazing that the man in the study next to mine still makes my heart lift when he passes my open door on the way to get another cup of coffee. That man is, of course, my husband, John. Turns out "Honey, I'm *still* home" is just how I want it.

And then there's Griffin, our Bouvier des Flandres. Right there with us, always connected by an unseen current of unconditional love.

I am the daughter of writers, and from an early age I swore to myself that I would never ever write a book. But I did look with wonderment at my parents when they edited each other's work with a coded language and an unspoken, shared aesthetic. I was let in on these moments in the kitchen, when my father would read aloud, perhaps a poem by John Donne, perhaps merely a newspaper article, as my mother cooked. I will always associate the sound of my father's voice and the almost audible quality to my mother's acute listening to the heady smell of dinner on the stove.

Los Angeles is the home of my dearest friend, Andrea Nevins. Andrea, David, Clara, Charlie, and Jesse are as dear to me as family, and their home has been my home away from home during my many research trips to Los Angeles. This book would not have been possible without their warm welcome. And it would not have been nearly as fun to write.

I collected two hundred recipes for this book. To get from two hundred to the best one hundred meant testing and retesting and debating an ever-shifting table of contents. Chrissy Tkac was by my side at every step on this book and on my last one. She is the dream intern. A cook who is both intuitive and trained, a perfectionist, a sublime baker, and a lovely friend.

Everyone needs an advocate and a protector. My friend and agent, Eric Simonoff, is that force. Eric and his wife, Meredith Kaffel Simonoff, are two of the best people I know.

Jenny Wapner, my editor, was the first to understand my fascination with the evolving food scene of Los Angeles and to support it. A native herself, she pushed for this book every step of the way with grace and determination, editing down to the wire, even as she was fast approaching the due date for her second child. Emma Rudolph, who stepped in seamlessly when Jenny went on maternity leave and, with a keen eye and generous disposition, helped take the book to the finish line. Jane Tunks Demel, a copy editor who is both delicate and precise, always pushing not only for accuracy but for a unified voice. And Aaron Wehner, the visionary behind Ten Speed Press. Aaron never fails to amaze me with his intuitive and confident aesthetic. How lucky to have him championing lasting quality in a world that too often cuts corners.

I've had the great luck of working with Creative Director Emma Campion on two books now, and both times, I've been awed by her ability to listen to my inchoate ramblings and envision a finished beauty. Emma had the good sense to pair me with photographer Ray Kachatorian, stylist Valerie Aikman-Smith, prop stylist Amy Paliwoda, and in-house designer Lisa Ferkel. No one could ask for a more talented, more committed team.

Publicity Director Kristin Casemore and I began chatting on the phone when I was still in graduate school. At the time, I was working as a field producer for Martha Stewart and came across a Ten Speed Press book that I wanted to feature. It was through Kristin that I fell in love with Ten Speed Press, and now here we are, all these years later, the conversation still on and still a pleasure.

Nearly every recipe in this book is being published for the first time. But, in a couple of instances, a recipe has been previously published, and I simply couldn't forgo including it. My thanks to those publishers who've generously given us permission to reprint a beloved recipe here and there, most notably Chronicle Books for letting me publish Travis Lett's recipes and Prospect Park Books for letting us include Christine Moore's oatcakes.

Which leads me finally to thank, last, but not at all least, the breathtakingly brilliant chefs who inspired me to write this book and who very generously helped me fill it with their tried-and-true recipes. This book is about you, and it is very much for you.

ABOUT THE AUTHOR

ALEKSANDRA CRAPANZANO is a screenwriter and food writer. A recipient of the M.F.K. Fisher Award for Distinguished Writing from the James Beard Foundation, she has been widely published in the *New York Times Magazine, Food & Wine, Saveur, Travel + Leisure, Gourmet, Elle, Departures,* and the *Wall Street Journal,* where for the last 8 years she's been a food columnist. Her essays have been anthologized, most notably in *Best American Food Writing,* and she is the author of *The London Cookbook: Recipes from the Restaurants, Cafés, and Hole-in-the-Wall Gems of a Modern City.* Aleksandra is married to the novelist John Burnham Schwartz. They live in New York with their son Garrick and dog Griffin.

INDEX

All rights reserved.
Published in the United States by Ten Speed Press,
an imprint of the Crown Publishing Group, a division of
Penguin Random House LLC, New York.
www.crownpublishing.com
www.tenspeed.com

Ten Speed Press and the Ten Speed Press colophon are registered
trademarks of Penguin Random House LLC.

Library of Congress Cataloging-in-Publication Data
Names: Crapanzano, Aleksandra, author.
Title: Eat, Cook, L.A. : notes and recipes from the City of Angels /
    Aleksandra Crapanzano.
Description: First edition. | California : Ten Speed Press,
    an imprint of the Crown Publishing Group, a division of
    Penguin Random House LLC, [2019] | Includes index.
Identifiers: LCCN 2018040643
Subjects: LCSH: International cooking. | Cooking—California—Los Angeles. |
    Restaurants—California—Los Angeles. | LCGFT: Cookbooks.
Classification: LCC TX725.A1 C644 2019 | DDC 641.59—dc23
LC record available at https://lccn.loc.gov/2018040643

Hardcover ISBN: 978-0-399-58047-5
eBook ISBN: 978-0-399-58048-2

Printed in China

Design by Lisa Ferkel
Food styling by Valerie Aikman-Smith
Prop styling by Amy Paliwoda
Props provided by The Surface Library

10 9 8 7 6 5 4 3 2 1

First Edition